"I remember sitting in my living ro‹     ɔy out of the invisible strings of the Un.    ...........ueu the method in her new book! My personal favorite sections are those on Sacred Technologies for the Absolute. Thanks, Tricia, for opening our hearts and eyes to what's real!"

PATTI GREEN
ENTREPRENEUR AND PRESIDENT OF VIRIDIS COMPANY, INC.

*"Absolute Joy* delivers exactly that ... as a real possibility for your life! Tricia Croyle's profound insights are expressed beautifully in her playful and brilliant storytelling. This book is packed with useful tools and quick ways to experience deep inner connections that lead to a life of absolute joy. You will delight in an abundance of easy-to-implement ideas that are wondrous and whimsical, yet practical and transforming."

NIKOLE KADEL
A FACILITATOR OF SPIRITUAL EXPANSION

"Tricia offers the reader an opportunity to discover how to become a master at harnessing the most powerful manifestation vibration of the Universe ... the Sacred Absolute. As you follow along you will learn how to wield this power to transform your life using her cutting-edge tools, processes, and exercises. If you're ready to take your spiritual practice to the next level ... this book is a must read!"

RIKKA ZIMMERMAN
A GLOBAL LEADER IN CONSCIOUSNESS

"Tricia is a master at dancing and weaving with energy. She plays with the energies of joy, love, abundance, and more with this beautiful gift of hers. In this, her latest book Tricia allows us the reader to go on this journey with her teaching us with various tools how to dance and weave ourselves through these energies. To live in the absolute Joy we are meant to be. I loved her openness about who she really is. She is not afraid to be this absolute joy, and I am reminded of the love and the joy of my own BEing when I read her beautifully crafted words. An absolute must read if you want to feel the Absolute Joy of life expressed to its fullest."

DEBBIE SHUMAN ESPINOZA
BEST SELLING AUTHOR, SPEAKER, WORTHINESS WARRIOR

# OTHER CREATIONS BY
# TRICIA JEANE CROYLE

**Books**

*From Heartache to Joy: One Woman's Journey Home*
*From Heartache to Joy: The Companion Playbook*
*Beyond Joy: A Journey into Freedom, Wisdom, Power, and Wellbeing*

**Cards**

*The Morning Prayer Cards*
*The Rose Path Meditation Cards*

**Free Gift**

Get a free gift for joining The Joy Project at www.heartachetojoy.com

# ABSOLUTE JOY:

## A JOURNEY BEYOND TIME TO NOWHERE

Tricia Jeane Croyle

**BALBOA.**PRESS

A DIVISION OF HAY HOUSE

Balboa Press books may be ordered through booksellers or by contacting:

Balboa Press
A Division of Hay House
1663 Liberty Drive
Bloomington, IN 47403
www.balboapress.com
1 (877) 407-4847

Print information available on the last page.

ISBN: 978-1-9822-4830-7 (sc)
ISBN: 978-1-9822-4831-4 (e)

Balboa Press rev. date: 06/23/2020

# CONTENTS

# FOREWORD

So many of us live our daily lives on **automatic pilot** ... Whenever we feel bored, depressed, or stuck in a rut, our attention has been drawn to notice that automatic pilot. In automatic pilot our lives follow schedules, habits, and timelines, based on norms that we have unconsciously picked up from other people, and from the world around us, be it culture, family, education, or media. Our days and weeks seem to be driven by those norms and schedules. Life can seem pointless and meaningless. We can lose motivation to do what used to bring enjoyment. We may even disbelieve in the reality of such concepts as joy, peace, harmony, and even love. When our life and our relationships feel flat, those words seem abstract and unattainable.

*Life sucks, and then you die* is a slogan I have heard from clients whom I guide in my Transformational Coaching & Energy Healing practice. For many, there is a pervasive perception that life is meaninglessness or hopeless. How many of us live right on the edge of depression? How many people fear that they might get pulled into the pit of despair ... and feel helpless to get off that slippery slope? How many people use medication or substances to manage their despondency—and to get a good sleep? This approach primarily addresses these states as chemical or neurological imbalances that require external intervention.

**But you, dear reader**, **have seen another option**. Because you have opened this unique book, *Absolute Joy: A Journey Beyond Time to Nowhere*, you have thereby opened yourself to a whole other universe—with guidance to live your life joyfully and playfully!

The underlying assumption woven through this, and Tricia Croyle's other books about Joy, is a profoundly empowering spiritual truth. I sum it up as this: *You always have choices at every moment and at every turn. AND your choices create your experience.* Once we understand this truth and act upon it, our perception of everything changes. One of my greatest joys as a Transformational Coach is when I witness clients come to the realization that the unconscious tunnel of limitation that they have been living within is actually **illusion**. The only awareness possible in these limiting tunnels of the automatic program is of the inherited beliefs and the self-judgments that limit. Upon shifting out of that dark tunnel, they see that they indeed have an infinite menu of conscious choices with which to create the flow of their own life! In the tunnel they did not know these choices even existed.

When we are empowered to consciously choose how we respond to life, we experience it very differently. When we know we can be in the driver's seat of our life, through choosing that which brings joy, fun, beauty, abundance, and love, then our perception and experience aligns with those choices. Tricia, both in her writing, and in her own living, unabashedly embraces her own unlimited access to conscious choice. And she unwaveringly accepts yours as well! This book is a celebration of the power of choice!

In *Absolute Joy*, Tricia explores and unpacks many qualities of perception and experience that we can choose for our lives. She brings both her deep wisdom and playful fun into these explorations—giving us "taste tests" to show us possibilities. Where else can one explore the textures, colors, movements, and sensations of peace, bliss, love, health, abundance, magic, purpose, alignment, joy, and more? Tricia openly shares her unique awareness and insights. You can pick any section, as I have, and find clarification and Tricia's unique reframing of these aspects and qualities of life, of Source, of truth. Choose the pathway you wish to enhance for yourself and you will find loads of inspiration—and perhaps a prying open of stuck beliefs that have held you back. Transformation beckons!

Another underlying assumption in this book is Tricia's extensive experience and knowledge about life force energy. "Energy flows where attention goes" is a foundational principle in the fields of Energy Healing. Tricia lives this. She shares her dreams, experiences, and experimentations of choosing specific vibrational frequencies, and then playfully directs these frequencies to create whatever she chooses. Surprises are guaranteed!

In addition, Tricia offers dozens of simple yet potent Sacred Technologies to explore. These are practical and often playful exercises that guide us into living our life with beauty and joy. They are immediately accessible—you can apply them right away, while you are reading. This is so refreshing in a world where the norms of spiritual practice have often been arduous forms of self-discipline requiring extensive time and effort!

What if your spiritual journey itself can be freeing and in easy flow? For example, have you ever practiced the art of receiving? Ooh, that one is tantalizing! Check it out!

This is not a book to be read through in one day. It is more like a unique reference book for life. A book that you keep handy and read a section or a chapter at a time. Reading this way and using the Sacred Technologies might well become your favorite joyous spiritual life practice. Enjoy!

LESLIE SANDRA BLACK
HEART AWAKENING TRANSFORMATIONAL
COACHING & ENERGY HEALING
WWW.HEARTAWAKENING.CA

# PREFACE

## From Eeyore to the Cheshire Cat

In 2014, I suffered a great deal of loss in a short period of time. I lost my mom, two horses, three dogs, and three cats. I had been taking care of my mother for three years. I had lost the rest of my family before that—John's mom (John is my husband), my brother, and my dad. My mother-in-law had lived with us for four years.

By the time I lost *my* mom, I needed to get away, and I was ready to travel. I felt a kind of freedom. I had a lot of suppressed grief. I went about my life thinking that I was happy. After all, I was generally a happy person. But somehow my spark was gone, and I didn't even know it. I had pasted *happy* onto *sad*.

I attended a conference in 2015 where the people called me "Eeyore" (the sad donkey character from the Winnie the Pooh books). I spent a year trying to rekindle my sparkle. Sadness was leaking out of me, like a faucet that just wouldn't stop dripping. That year I discovered that it was necessary to allow myself to feel the grief and sadness so as to get through to the other side, which is Joy.

Then I had a pivotal experience. I called it the Joy Experience. I describe this experience in the beginning of chapter 2, "Absolute Joy."

## The Smile of the Cheshire Cat

My Joy Experience gave birth to my Cheshire Cat smile. It seemed like I became just a smile, and nothing else. When I approached people, they saw the smile.

I was attending an architecture conference, speaking to a log home vendor about logs for a possible architecture project in Northern California when he said to me, "I just have to tell you, you have the most beautiful smile."

Then the following year at another conference, I walked into an evening buffet and drinks, a social hour. I sat down at a table and began a conversation with a young man. "Hi. How are you? Why are you here?"

It was that kind of chitchat conversation that occurs when people first meet.

After a few minutes, the young man said, "Wow! How can I be you? I want to be you. I want your life."

Fast forward to the evening of another architecture conference when I was sitting near the vendors. I had been researching a project I was working on in Maine—a passive, zero-energy house I was designing for a friend. I overheard a conversation a little way up the aisle from where I was sitting. It went like this. "You need to meet this woman. She is the most amazing woman. You just got to meet her."

The conversation went on.

I thought, *Boy, I need to meet this person they are discussing.* The one man saw me sitting there and motioned me over. He wanted to introduce me to the person he was talking to. And then it occurred to me. They were talking about me! OMG! They were talking about me. I walked over to meet his friend and then just walked away and shook my head. I wondered when I went from being Eeyore to having the smile of the Cheshire Cat, becoming a woman with a beautiful smile and someone somebody else wanted to be or to meet.

# ACKNOWLEDGMENTS

I would like to thank my husband of fifty-plus years, for his perseverance in fighting the good fight for clean water and our environment. Also for allowing me to be me. For allowing me to take the time I need to write.

I thank Rikka Zimmerman for giving me the opportunity to share my true nature on a larger stage.

I thank my fellow Life Transformed coaches for encouraging me to put myself out there.

I thank Leslie Sandra Black for being a true friend, and for keeping me going when I got stuck.

I would like to thank my editor Nina Shoroplova for turning my ramblings into a kind of sense that people can read and understand. And for her encouragement to keep going.

I would like to thank all my coaches, guides, and animal friends that constantly remind me to keep on my path.

# INTRODUCTION

 Sometimes God hands you a book and you had better write it!

## The Joy Series

This is the third book in The Joy Series, part of a project I call, The Joy Project.

### *From Heartache to Joy: One Woman's Journey Home*

In the first book, *From Heartache to Joy: One Woman's Journey Home*, I explored my journey in discovering who I am and how I have allowed myself to come out into the world as an authentic being. I shared my Morning Prayer and the exercises that developed out of that practice. I called these energies (sometimes referred to as feelings) *aspects of God* or the Source of the Universe. Each aspect as I explored it became a pathway to explore myself and the energy that surrounded me as I explored it.

My first book identified fifteen aspects of God Source, all of which, like spokes on a wheel, afford a path inward to the center of our being. Each aspect comprised a chapter.

### *Beyond Joy: A Journey into Freedom, Wisdom, Power and Wellbeing*

As I began to play with and explore the energies more and more, new aspects emerged, and I wrote the second book, *Beyond Joy: A Journey into*

*Freedom, Wisdom, Power and Wellbeing.* This book was a continuation of the exploration of the aspects of our God Source, with the addition of another twelve aspects, ranging from *Breath* to *Wonder.* In this book I added to the aspects, the conditions that we are surrounded by and the tools that we use. This second book in the series became much more of a *how to* book because it became apparent that people wanted to know how I had gone beyond the transformation of my sadness and grief into a Joyful being. I had gone beyond playing in the energy of Joy to the point where I could weave and dance with that energy.

## From Heartache to Joy: The Companion Playbook

I wrote *From Heartache to Joy: The Companion Playbook* to accompany the first book. It offers more and expanded exercises than the first book. It is full of exercises, puzzles, and quizzes, and is meant as a workbook. I call it a playbook because I don't believe we can work our way to Joy. It is an oversized book for journaling.

## Absolute Joy: A Journey Beyond Time to Nowhere

No longer were people calling me the *Cheshire Cat* instead of *Eeyore.* But now they were calling me the *Joy Magnet, Energy Dancer, Energy Weaver,* and most recently, *Dream Weaver of Worlds.* This ability to dance and weave pure energies is the result of experiencing absolute energy, *Absolute Joy.*

This book is about continuing to explore my path of *Absolute Joy.* It is also a journey of divine right timing to nowhere and to nothing.

In this third book in The Joy Series, *Absolute Joy,* I came to each of these pathways or aspects through direct experience by extensive practice of what I call the Morning Prayer, as well as through the exercises I have shared. A complete Morning Prayer can be found in the Appendix section at the end of this book. Most of the techniques are my own exercises, which came to me during meditations.

**The Rose Path Meditations**

Throughout the book you will find sayings or quotes marked with a rose. These are meant to give you pause so you can think about them throughout your day. They are marked with a rose because that is the way that I thank my guides for their help—I give each one a rose. I also give roses to my animal guides. It is simply the way I say, *Thank you.*

Some time ago, my guides started giving me roses in return—they saw fit to scatter roses on my path. So that is the way I find my path. I look for and smell the roses. And I give these roses to you. Each petal is meant to give you pause. To stop and smell. Sometimes, it is readily apparent why it is there. And sometimes, you will have to think about it. They are a little like "koans." You are meant to meditate upon them.

# The Cards

I created *The Morning Prayer Cards* and *The Rose Path Meditation Cards* to supplement the first two books. They can be found on my website, www. heartachetojoy.com. *The Morning Prayer Cards* are meant to accompany the first book. There twenty-eight cards each with an animal to represent the twenty-eight aspects. And *The Rose Path Meditation Cards* (seventy-eight cards in the deck) can accompany both the first two books. Both sets of cards would also work well with this third book in The Joy Series.

# God and the Universe

When I refer to God, I am also referring to Source or the Universe. I have also tried using the word, *Force.* As in "May the force be with you." I do not have a picture of God in my mind as if He were a deity or even masculine. I intend only to refer to the Source of us all. I find it easiest to use the word *God.* If this disturbs you, please substitute *Source* or any other word you feel is appropriate. The use of the word God works well when I talk about many of the aspects. The use of Universe works better when I talk about the conditions; and Force works when I am describing the energy. They are all meant to be interchangeable.

🌹 Our books read us. When we reread
them, we are in a different place.

## How to Read This Book

It is not necessary that you read the chapters or practice the techniques in this book in any order. Any path home to yourself is the right one. Pick the aspect—the chapter—that resonates with you. Read that chapter or any part of that chapter, and practice the technique associated with it for as long as you need to. Then try another one. Try these techniques from the being who you currently are. If one chapter doesn't seem to work, that's okay. Move on to the next one. They will aid you in letting go of struggle, and assist you with stepping into that Absolute Joy, just as they aided me.

Each chapter is seen through the lens of all or most of the other chapters. In that regard, if you understood one chapter, you would understand all the others. So, you could do one chapter really well and not do the others. Chapter 13 gathers all the techniques together in one place. Since there are twelve other chapters, you might find that reading one a month suits you. Write in your journal what transpires.

This book offers tools and techniques for integrating all energies. Some of the techniques at the end of the chapters are in addition to what is described in the chapter. The exercises offer a kind of spiritual technology. Hence, I call them Sacred Technologies.

It is my intention to inspire, to support, and to celebrate your experience as you struggle, overcome, and discover the *Absolute Joy* in living your journey.

Authentically yours,
Tricia Jeane Croyle, AIA, BA, BED, MOB, ALTC

# CHAPTER 1

# THE ABSOLUTE

*The mind once expanded to the dimensions of larger ideas never returns to its original size.*

—OLIVER WENDELL HOLMES SR.

## Absolutely Absolute

*Dream: The Flying Saucer*

> *A small object about the size of a coffee cup saucer is flying around. I think to fly with it. So, I fly alongside it. Up and down, and all around we fly. Darting here and there. It is like a flying saucer drone. I wonder how it would be to fly with it when it goes to warp speed, and then disappears. Can I follow it then, and where would we end up? I know I will try. But maybe I'm not ready, and then I wake up.*

The Absolute is a pure and unquestionable principle. It is absolute power. What would it be like to jump on that flying saucer drone?

There are no if, ands, or buts in the Absolute. It is everywhere, and a direct line at the same time. It is total awareness with the direct line and focus of intention. The absolute is like being a part of God, and separate at the same time. It is a drop of water recognizing itself while still being in the ocean. We sometimes call this *awareness*, the sea of awareness, and we are that drop of water.

So how does that drop of water come to have an absolute focus? That is unwavering intent. Our peripheral vision sees the distractions of life, but our intent is steadfast in our choice to walk a direct path. Even if that path seems to be wandering and not so direct.

### No Matter What

We live our lives going in a certain direction. No matter what. Things pop up to try to stop us. Or are they just the scenery that we wave to in acknowledgment as we drive by on the freeway? "No matter what" is such a funny phrase. *Matter* has substance but when we say, *no matter*, that thing has no substance. So, nothing of substance stops us. We simply go on our way.

## Absolute through the Aspects

I have chosen Absolute Joy as my path. Or has it chosen me? When it is absolute, there is no separation between the path and the walker on the path. What we walk is a reflection of us and who we are. What you see is what you think about whether you intend to think about it or not.

Consciousness is being aware of what you are thinking. If you don't want to think it, then change your thought, and choose what you do want to think. I choose to think and feel Joy. So, if I find that my thoughts are not in alignment with Joy, then I change my alignment by changing my thoughts, and I put myself back on my chosen path. How I go about doing this is the subject matter of this book, *Absolute Joy*. The Absolute is about allowance, totality, and unconditionality.

*Absolute Peace* is about total allowance, quiet, and harmony. *Absolute Love* is about unconditional love and total allowance. *Absolute Abundance* is about the realization that it already exists, and the acceptance of the infinite abundance that is already here. *Absolute Healing* is about stepping into the perfect health that is, and accepting whatever is occurring with your body and mind at the same time. *Absolute Gratitude* is stepping into the wonder of the world around us and acknowledging it for everything that is happening with the wonder of a little girl skipping on a sidewalk.

*Absolute Magic* is stepping into the unknown and allowing it to remain unknown. *Absolute Co-Creation* is not looking left or right, but only looking at the next step on your path. Focus, intention, and awareness at the same time. *Absolute Divine Perfection* is waiting and accepting the divine right time and the right place for things to occur, and acknowledging that God knows better than we do for what is the next right thing to happen. *Absolute Purpose* is being aware of our path, acknowledging the path, and walking the path no matter what. *Absolute Energy* is standing in the primordial soup of infinite possibility that we sometimes call space, and choosing an energy to stand in.

*Sacred Technologies of the Absolute* are the exercises, techniques, and practices that can bring us home to ourselves where all of the aspects of the absolute reside. I call them sacred because they are connected to God and the Universe. They are the pure and unquestionable principles that allow us to experience life as it flows through us.

Any one of these aspects from Joy to Energy, if practiced and lived absolutely, would lead you to all the others. If you really lived in absolute Joy, you would already be also living in absolute Peace and absolute Love. One cannot live in any of these absolutely without also living in all the others. If you are absolutely any of these aspects, you will also be absolutely all of them. The Absolute is like the flying saucer drone. You would go at warp speed to Joy or Peace, and to all that is.

## Interaction of Common Aspects

Each chapter is an aspect of God, or a condition of the Universe or tool that is available to us. They are all also pathways. For this third book, I have chosen twelve of the most common Aspects that most of my students ask questions about or take classes on. To explore how these aspects impact our lives and my own life, I combined the various tools, aspects, and conditions.

*Energy Organizational Chart*

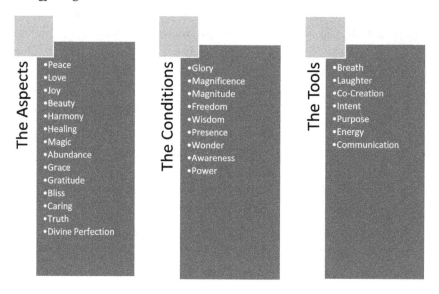

The Aspects
- Peace
- Love
- Joy
- Beauty
- Harmony
- Healing
- Magic
- Abundance
- Grace
- Gratitude
- Bliss
- Caring
- Truth
- Divine Perfection

The Conditions
- Glory
- Magnificence
- Magnitude
- Freedom
- Wisdom
- Presence
- Wonder
- Awareness
- Power

The Tools
- Breath
- Laughter
- Co-Creation
- Intent
- Purpose
- Energy
- Communication

Let me explain what I mean by "I combined the various tools, aspects, and conditions."

During my morning meditation today, my word was *Energy.* That isn't even one of my Morning Prayer words. But at the writing of this book, it became one. The word, *Energy,* got me thinking about the structural organization of the words I currently use as aspects of God.

I call all the *feeling* words *aspects of God.* Aspects are like the colors that make up the rainbow, with the Universe being the rainbow. The conditions are what surround us. The tools are what we use to deal with these conditions. So, the Organizational Chart for Energy looks like this.

## The Aspects

The aspects are something that we feel. We become these energies. We feel these energies. We are the Peace that we see. As an energy, an aspect has a color and a flavor. It can be a tool. We can use that energy to foster more Peace. But the tools are not something that we generally become. We don't become *communication* or *laughter.* They are tools that we use to become more of our aspect energy. The conditions are something that surrounds us. We act from presence or power. We stand in their midst.

*Power* seems like a tool, but it is a fuel and reinforces the other tools and the aspects. It fuels Peace and it makes our intent stronger.

So, what about *energy*? That was today's word. I put it in the category of tool. I use it all the time. I play in it. But I give it a color or flavor like the flavor of Peace. Which for me is blue. Pale blue like the sky. And maybe the flavor of blueberries. Very subtle. Or is it *berry subtle*? Ha! I can place the various conditions around it, like *awareness* or *power*. Peace in awareness or peace in power. Both of those are beautiful conditions to hang out in. So today I will notice where Peace is fueled by Power and hang out in the energy of that place.

Then I asked myself the question of how the aspects interact with each other. Like how does the tool of *Breath* interact with the aspect of our *Health*, or how does the tool of *Power* interact with the aspect of *Joy*? I discuss the Power of Joy not the Joy of having power. Or how our Joy allows us to Co-Create.

*Absolute Joy* is about the interactions of the paths. When we understand how the aspects interact with each other, we are better able to understand how the purity of the energy of that aspect exists in its absolute form.

I call the book *Absolute Joy*, because if you only understood that you could stand in pure Joy, no matter what, the game would be over. There would be nothing to fix or change. Everything would be easy because everything is already done. You would understand that there is nothing to do but experience your path of *Absolute Joy*. It is *a journey beyond time to nowhere*.

 *We edit our lives in the same way we edit our books.*

## Absolute through Edit

When we edit a book, there is a structural edit, a copy edit, and a proof edit. We edit our lives in a similar way. The proof edit is like absolute health. It is closer to perfect. The structural edit is similar to *what* we do in life. The copy edit is similar to *how* we perform in life. We edit our lives through our intention.

Words carry energy beyond their meanings as found in a dictionary or used by the people. I strive for authenticity, which is its own kind of truth. I know that people will receive whatever they need to step forward on their own personal journey as I have done on mine. The Universe is always in charge, and I trust in it.

*Absolute Joy* is a stream-of-consciousness tour of my own transformational journey. By sharing this tour, and the experiences I had along the pathway, I hope that you will discover your own pathway home to yourself. I have begun each chapter with a story, dream, journey, vision, or meditation. I share them because they are the way that my subconscious and conscious minds become integrated. This integration colors the way I perceive the world. I also incorporate the ideas from various books I have read and classes I have attended. There is a list of books and spiritual practitioners in the resources section at the end of the book.

## Absolute through My Practices

*The Morning Prayer and the Joy of Co-Creating Joy*

I sat in meditation this morning especially grateful. I was grateful for the usual things but also grateful for my coffee, the tablecloth on the dining room table, the box of Kleenex, and just being alive. My gratitude seemed deeper, and I slowed down my Morning Prayer, and thought about it. I spent a few seconds on each of the words.

I started this practice way back in 2014 with the words *Peace, Love,* and *Joy.* That is all there was in my world of Morning Prayer. Then I added *Beauty.* It just seemed to follow. I looked at all the beauty in the world. Then *Harmony* made sense. Because a beautiful world also had harmony in it, and what did that mean? How was everything in harmony? Harmony was followed by *Grace.* Defined by a movement in grace. Not just what we are aligned to but how we move into it with grace. And then there was *Healing.* When we stop moving and stop doing all things, healing can take place.

What is next? *Communication.* When we ask the question, we are in communication with all that is, with people, animals, and the Universe. So how do we do that? That was the next question that I asked, and then an *Abundance* flowed through me. The abundance of all that is. We can experience all that is, and then we are grateful. *Gratitude* flows through us. Gratitude naturally follows from the experience of abundance.

I began to see that there was an order that the words came in. That the order wasn't arbitrary, and that it was meant to be that way. *Magic* follows gratitude. That makes sense because gratitude is the catalyst for all magic. I knew that. And then came *Bliss*. Having experienced the magic of the universe, we fall into bliss, and then I can't remember what comes next, and that also makes sense because who would want to leave bliss? There doesn't seem to be anything else.

That is the *Truth*, and truth follows. The truth leads us to recognizing Divine Perfection. Once we see divine perfection everywhere, we are able to co-create, and we discover *Co-Creation*. We co-create with the Universe. Each one of those words became a chapter in *From Heartache to Joy*, and they were in that order.

But then I continued on. However, these new words added the conditions, and tools to the aspects. The first group of words were the feelings, and colors of Love. The next were the conditions we found ourselves in, and the tools to get out of the opposite of those conditions as well as some more aspects. What's next? The *Power* and the *Glory*. Once we Co-Create, we do step into power and we can celebrate with the glory.

It is *Magnificent*, and has the Magnitude of everywhere and nowhere. Then the tools appeared—the *Breath* and *Caring* mixed with the condition of the *Freedom* that ensues. Our *Intent*, which is our focus. *Laughter* appears. Can we laugh at ourselves and the universe? Are we present in this moment? *Presence*. Then we gain the *Wisdom* of the Universe, and begin to *Wonder* about what else there is. We ask, *What shall I notice today?*

All of this took just a few moments.

What I saw today was the magnificent organization in the ordering of the words. Power through Wonder was my second book, *Beyond Joy*. To those I added purpose and awareness, which are added to this book, *Absolute Joy*.

I thought about this before I drew my prayer cards, and then I drew them. I drew the card of the Morning Prayer itself. The one with the prayer on it. I left that card in the deck as an explanation. It serves much like a

Joker card, so that people would know how to use the prayer cards. Then I drew *Co-Creation* and *Joy*.

I don't need to draw from the deck of cards. After all I created them, and I can certainly simply ask the question, *What shall I meditate on today?* But I think that playing with the cards is fun.

## Centering and Writing

One of the commenters from my blog this morning asked about centering herself or maybe it was a himself. He/she didn't want to waste the fifteen minutes it took to center in order to start writing. I think that my reply is relevant here because it is about the Joy of Co-Creation. It's about being in Joy when we Co-Create with God, and we are at our center where God also resides.

*How do we center ourselves?* is an interesting question. I think that the question for writers is how to focus a muddled mind. How to get rid of all the other thoughts that are coming up in order to focus on what we believe we are supposed to be writing. It's true that I have a routine, and I will share that routine with you. But I think the more important question is this: *Why do you have the muddled mind?*

In my own case I have nothing to write about, until I do. Sometimes when I meditate, I am so filled with ideas that I can't wait to write them down. Other times, there seems to be nothing. I sit down to write anyway and my fingers just start typing. Maybe it's drivel that comes out. I don't know. But when I read what I have written I say, *Hmmm that's interesting,* and *How about this?*

*Center* is a funny word. When I think of centering, I think of going into zero point. Zero point is the true center for all that is, and it is in our center. To center, I actually step into that place where there is nothing and take a look around, and say to myself and the Universe, *What of the infinite possibility from here do I choose to be a part of and participate in today?* Sometimes I write about that.

*Grounding*

Or I ground and use grounding energy to kick start my brain and heart-mind into writing about something that I believe might be of benefit to humanity. It might be something amazing, something funny, or something that would change a person's perception of the world in a good way. If I have a mission, it is to spread the Joy that I see into the world. So, if one of my ideas can do that, I write about it. I want to leave the world a better place than I found it.

I don't think that any of us needs fixing or changing. But I believe that others believe that they do. That is why they come to my website and read my blogs in the first place. It is their belief that they need fixing and changing. Change your perception and you change your life.

Change your perception about not being already centered. Realize you are centered and you change your life. Change your idea that the fifteen minutes is wasted. What if it's not wasted? And guess what also happens? You are happy during that fifteen minutes and the fifteen minutes also goes away.

Acceptance of *what is* changes into what we wish it to be. The fifteen minutes just might go away. Or not. Either way, you are happier and writing from a place of being centered.

*My Practice*

Every morning I rise with the sun and greet it. I say my Morning Prayer. You can find a copy of the prayer in the appendix. I start with gratitude. It is impossible to overdo being grateful. I am grateful for being alive and for the day I am about to experience.

Then I ask, *What shall I experience today? What aspect of God source should I see reflected in every breath and step I take?* Then I listen. I usually hear a word or start thinking about an idea.

This week, I selected three cards instead of one from my Morning Prayer Card deck because I wanted the complexity of the ideas. Today I selected Breath, Abundance, and Love. I had intended to write about how Abundance is a color or aspect of Love. And how Love is the absence but yet the possibility of all that is. And how Breath is a tool to access that Love, which would inform us of our state of Abundance energy. The Breath is an excellent tool for all things. In fact, it is a good tool for centering.

So, if your mind is muddled, focus on your breath. Be grateful for your breath, and breathe in and out ten times counting to seven on the in and out breaths. Make your breath circular. Do not hold it in at the top or the bottom of your breath. Focus on your breath and nothing else.

Then start writing or doing whatever it is that you choose to do the rest of your day.

## Sacred Technologies of the Absolute

1. **No Matter What.** Say: *No matter what, I am absolute* ... (fill in the blank with an energy like Joy, Peace, or Love). You can also say, *No matter what I am*, and then say nothing. That is even more absolutely absolute.

2. **Morning Prayer.** Pick one word for the day, and look for that aspect, condition, or tool throughout your day.

3. **Align** yourself with the day's word. The word will align you with your path. Check throughout your day. Are you still noticing that word?

4. **Choose.** Say three times: *I now choose to stay on my path, no matter what.*

5. **Centering.** Focus on your breath. Be grateful for your breath. Breathe in and out ten times counting to seven on the in and the out breaths. Make your breath circular. Do not hold it in at the top or the bottom of your breath. Focus on your breath and nothing else.

6. **Focus.** Notice your noticing. Play with focus and fuzzy awareness within the act of noticing. Go from laser focus to fuzzy awareness. Go back and forth. Can you do both at the same time? What are you noticing right now?

# CHAPTER 2

# ABSOLUTE JOY

 *I don't have to bring in Joy. I just have to stop repressing it.*

## The Joy Experience

*The sunrise over the Bimini flats at the marina is spectacular. It would be impossible not to feel its magnificence. Pink, lavender, and gold finger the aqua sea. I am in such gratitude. I am thankful for being alive, and for each breath of air. For the retreat I am attending. For the couch I am sitting on. For the sparkling water and the sunrise.*

*I ask God, "Show me how much Joy I can possibly be. How much Joy can God be through me?"*

*I wait, and now I am showered with a billion sparkles of light. I feel my body explode out into the Universe as those sparkles of Joy. Will I come back together again? Or will I remain as a billion pieces of light out in the Universe? I come back together. Now, I wonder if I can walk.*

*As I get up to leave, I stand up, and the ground not only supports me, but it is giggling as I walk on it. Now I wonder if I can eat, and swallow food. I go into the buffet at the hotel, and the food tastes exquisite. Even the water is exquisite. I run up to people, and say, "I am so full of Joy that I can't contain it."*

*They say, "Don't contain it."*
*So, I don't. I share it.*
*And I am still sharing it today.*

The above experience happened as I was greeting the morning sunrise on February 15, 2016, in Bimini, and saying my Morning Prayer (see Appendix). At the time there were just three pathways to God (Universe) in my experience: Peace, Love, and Joy. The other aspects, conditions, and tools to come home to ourselves came later.

I can relive that experience any time I choose, although it is different each time. I can simply go to that place of exquisite joy, and feel the billion sparkles of light that I am. It is different now because I am a different person than I was. I now perceive it differently. But it is also still very powerful.

We can never go back. We are different, and there is only the present moment anyway. Some have said that this was a *samadhi* experience. I would say that maybe that is so. I am less concerned with what I call it than I am with how to experience it. I would ask what if we could have this state in every moment and with every breath? Some might say that then we would be enlightened. But what if it is just Absolute Joy? What if we are just living our life in Absolute Joy? And maybe Absolute Joy is just the name I have given the experience.

*The purpose of art is washing the dust of daily life off our souls.*

—Pablo Picasso

## The Joy of Joy

Picasso talks about the dust of daily life on our souls. It is my intention with what I call The Joy Project to do just that. To wash that dust off all our souls. I do it with the art form of story. I tell a story, and it resonates with the audience. It is the vibration of that resonance that shakes the dust off.

It is the Joy of joy that is absolute Joy. When joy creates more joy creates more joy. That is pure Joy. Merriam Webster says that *Joy* is "the

12

emotion evoked by wellbeing, success, or good fortune or by the prospect of possessing what one desires." But that dictionary definition is conditional. Joy is conditioned on health or wealth or the fulfillment of a desire. First, we will look at Joy as a condition of those things. Then in each chapter there will be a section about Joy not being conditioned on those things, but those things being conditioned on Joy. What if the reverse is also true? What if it is also true that Joy brings us wealth, health, and the things that we desire? And what if Joy could be conditioned on choice? And what if that choice were to live a life of *Absolute Joy?*

## Joy through Health

The Joy of health is easy. Of course, good health brings us Joy. If we don't have good health, we often ask, what good is Wealth or Peace or Love? We can't enjoy them if our health is bad. So, good health brings us or allows us to experience Joy. But if our health is bad, can we still have Joy? Yes. Of course. Joy is a choice regardless of health. But with good health, we don't have a difficult time choosing Joy. It's easy. When we are grateful for something that we already have, then that gratitude acts as a catalyst for Joy. Good health makes it easy to take and stay on the path of Joy.

Disease or pain takes our mind and attention down a different path from Joy. Disease, if we allow it, takes us further down the path of disease. Pain can consume our mind and attention to the point where it can occupy our actions so that we stay in bed, sit on the couch, or watch mindless television. So good health makes it easier to get and stay on the path of Joy.

Health makes the expression of Joy fun. It is easier with good health to dance, love, laugh, sing, and create Joy.

Want more Joy? Get more health. Then experience the Joy of health.

## Joy through Abundance

Many of us believe that we would be happier if only we had more money. More wealth, more abundance. It is the wanting that takes us out of Joy. Wanting is not the energy of abundance or Joy. Wanting says that we are not whole and complete, that something is missing from our life. We believe we would be happy if that missing thing were here. What is missing is contentment and satisfaction. To have Joy we need to be content with what we have. We need to be satisfied with who we are and where we work or don't work.

Of course, we are happy if we win the lotto or get a raise at work. But that happiness is conditional, and only lasts a short time. Then we find that we are asking, *What is next? What else is there?* Asking those questions is okay. But asking them from the place of *What I have right now is good* and *What else is there?* is even better. When we ask from that place, we can expect that much more abundance will flow to us. It flows because we are asking from a place of Abundance. The emotion evoked by wellbeing, success, or good fortune or by the prospect of possessing what one desires creates the energy of having. Abundance flows to abundance. Like attracts like. Abundance flows to the energy of *having*. Being in Joy about what one already has is the highest energy of having.

## Joy through Love

I discovered the Joy of Love in relationships through hugging. I now call my hugging, *the hug of zero point*. I used not even to hug. In fact, I hated the thought of hugging people other than my family. When I went up to hug someone I was greeting, I felt very uncomfortable. I cringed inwardly. I didn't really see the point. Any of those who have experienced my hugs recently will find this hard to believe. So, what changed?

### *The Hug*

It started with a hug in Hawaii. I was at a spiritual retreat. Most people were greeting others with hugs. But not me. So, I spoke to a spiritual leader there, and I asked him how to hug. I told him I didn't understand hugging, and I didn't know how to hug. He gave me a hug to show me, and he said, *Breathe. Just breathe.* So, I did. It was okay.

Then what happened was that I began to breathe as I gave a hug. Over time I began to breathe into myself. The idea of hugging began to change, and I began to enjoy it. Then I began to breathe the other person. I stayed there for a while and hung out in the hug. I breathed the other person, and then I breathed myself.

I went back and forth breathing the other and myself. Back and forth. Then the hug became really interesting. Energy was moving, and I was swaying with the energy, and the other person began swaying also. At one point I felt as if we were two palm trees swaying in the breeze. I got comments from the other person like *That was really wonderful. It was so peaceful* or *so joyful,* and *I love your hugs.*

*Witness to Joy*

I also began to love my hugs. I went even deeper into the process as the breath of the other person and my own breath became one breath, and then I breathed God. After that I went right away to the breath of God. When I was going to hug someone, I went into breathing God, and I watched as things happened. Sometimes people received Peace or sometimes Joy or sometimes Bliss. I didn't receive that, or maybe I did, and I noticed what they received. I was given the gift of witnessing what they received. I didn't give it. God did. I just noticed it and witnessed what was given. Or sometimes not. I simply felt peaceful or wonderful.

Now I love to give hugs. I call it the *Hug of Zero Point.* Because when you go into nothing, all things are possible. That is where all healing occurs. I could call it the hug of Love. But that doesn't seem right even though it is true.

Sometimes we hate something, and we wrestle with the idea of it. That thing often becomes our greatest strength. That is certainly what happened to me with hugging, overcoming the distaste of hugging to the point where hugging for me now is absolute Joy.

## Joy through Peace

When we stand in peace, we can find Joy. Why is that? Peace fills us with quiet. We are removed from distractions. Merriam Webster defines *peace* as freedom from disturbance. Wikipedia defines *peace* as a concept of "societal friendship, and harmony in the absence of hostility, and violence.

In a social sense, peace is commonly used to mean a lack of conflict (such as war)." So, when there is an absence of hostility and violence and we stand in quiet, what do we choose? We can choose anything we want. I choose Joy. Does Peace bring us Joy? No, it is the absence of the non-peace that brings us the Joy.

## Bliss, Beauty, and Power

Bliss and beauty are entwined in how we use Power. How we use Power can determine how we entertain struggle.

Bliss is a very refined energy. It is a lot like Joy but there is less movement, and it is more like an infinite ball exploding out in all directions infinitely. The expansion is infinite in time and space.

Beauty is when you see or hear something, and that something grips your heart and makes you want to cry because it is so beautiful. Beauty is personal, and what we consider beautiful is in the eyes of the beholder.

Power in the spiritual energy sense and true power is *of* something or someone, and not *over* something or someone. By that I mean that true power is the potential energy to influence or move something without actually doing it. Although actually influencing or moving something is also power. Something moving or influencing something else is power *over*. Power *of* is the potential to move something.

A beautiful or charismatic person has power. Beauty and charisma have power. A bully has power over. The power of beauty influences us. The power of a bully enslaves us, and we struggle against it. We don't struggle against the power of beauty. We allow it to influence us and bring us into Joy.

## Duality

I am reminded of the lightworker Katrina Chaudoir who told me that Cheetah would be there for me to aid me in staying on my path. I believe that has to do with speed and power. The world is moving very rapidly. It is mired in a divisive energy, with the energy of duality. We think of this energy of duality as dividing us. It doesn't have to.

We could call on this energy instead to heal the planet and our fellow humans on it. Our plant and animal friends don't suffer from duality.

We suffer because we believe that we are separate. We are not. And that misbelief leads to the perception of the duality of everything. Love and hate. Peace and struggle. Beauty and ugliness. Powerfulness and weakness. Joy and sadness. We have even given the other side of duality's sword a name, and we have given it an identity of its own. But those negative energies don't need identities. We could simply Love and be in Peace. The opposite of Love is no Love, or of Beauty is no Beauty, not ugliness. Ugliness doesn't exist.

What if a person were struggling when they came up to us. And what if we said, *I am sorry that you are struggling*, and we stood in Peace as we said it. We don't have to join them in their struggling. We could simply offer Peace. When we stand in peace, at least we are no longer struggling. And then what happens, sometimes they join us there. The world becomes a more peaceful place one or two people at a time.

The world is in a divisive energy. Or is it really? What if it isn't, and we chose instead to see the world as a beautiful place with no struggling? What if we stepped into the Power of a Beautiful world, instead of an ugly, divisive world? What if no duality really exists but we are simply pretending that it does?

## Stand in the Opposite

When someone of a political party that we don't agree with says something awful that does not make us feel good, what if we said, *I'm sorry you feel that way* or *I am happy that political action works for you, and to your benefit*, and we stand there, in Peace? We Stand in … whatever is the opposite of what is being offered. If it is fear, then we stand in courage. If it is hatred, then we stand in Love. If it is struggle, then we stand in Peace. What a peaceful and pleasant world it would be!

We can do this out loud or we can do this silently. Sometimes even in our families (or maybe especially in our families), we can't express the differences in our political opinions at this time. If we can't do it with respect and love out loud, then we can do it with respect and love silently. But we must do it. We must stand in the power of our Love, Peace, and

Beauty that is the world. The real world. Not the made-up world of hate and division.

There is Joy in the world. There can be a walk in the *garden of joy*. We can have a *joy quest*. We can have a *joy road,* a *joy ride,* and we can unleash the Joy of the soul where we find Bliss.

## Joy through Gratitude

*Happy Holiday Giving*

> *Rikka Zimmerman comes up to me and says, "You look great!" and I say, "thank you, and you look," and I pause and close my eyes, and I say … "You don't look at all! and that's great." She smiles.*

*No Look*

Rikka Zimmerman is a leader in global consciousness, the creator of the Life Transformed coaching program that I study. What I mean by that is that Rikka has no look. Not great and yet great at the same time. Yes, from one perspective she looks great. But from another, she isn't even here. Not being here is not a bad thing. She's not absent or uncaring. It's that she cares so much that she can be all things to all people. So, whenever anyone looks at her, they see what they want to see or expect to see. They see someone beautiful or accomplished or talented or giving or … whatever. That Rikka has no look is the result of extreme evolutionary enlightenment.

*Our Gifts*

Then I think about myself and my own journey to that place of being all things. Where does it begin? For many it starts with being beautiful or accomplished or successful. Looks and talents are a given, literally. Our looks and talents are given to us at birth. It is up to us to use the gifts we are given. Everything we are given is a gift by definition. It is important to remember that, especially at gift-giving times of the year, like Christmas time. I am appalled at the advertising I see for gifts on television. The commercialization of a giving time of the year seems disrespectful, and out of tune with what is meant by giving and receiving.

### Giving and Receiving

Giving must be heartfelt. Receiving must also be heartfelt. They must be equal and opposite. My ability to give is much easier than my ability to receive. It usually has to do with worthiness, and a sense of guilt around already having too much and my judgment that there is not enough in the world. There are still vestiges of lack in my ego mind. Sometimes I let the feelings of lack control my ability to receive graciously and with love in my heart. So, at those times, I take a deep breath and let it all go. I say, *Thank you for this wonderful and thoughtful gift. I thank you from the depths of my heart.* No matter what the gift is. It is a gift.

I gave cookies, candy, and homemade cherry bounce last Christmas, as well as my books and meditation cards. I tell myself that even though the cookies are made of butter, sugar, and flour, they are also made with love. They are the recipes of my late Swedish mother-in-law, and they are superb! And it is the love that I am giving. They also honor her memory.

So, take a deep breath when you celebrate the holidays with your friends and family. Be the gracious love of giving and receiving. After all, you already are the gracious love of giving. You are the gift. Let go of the hustle and bustle and celebrate the Joy in simply being with friends and family. Celebrate in the Joy of just being alive.

## Joy through Magic

When we say "make believe," we refer to children playing their games. They are playing make believe. I use that phrase to describe "magic." We see magic when we believe it. We are making our beliefs come true by believing them, and that is magic.

Most things out there tend to bring me Joy. But magic is easy. It really brings me Joy. I don't have to look for the joy in it. It just is. I'm not a pixie-dust-and-fairy kind of person. But I do like fairies, and I think pixie dust is great.

## Magic Dust

I've learned to sprinkle pixie dust on my food when I give thanks before a meal. That is a good thing. Although I am forgetful about doing it. Sprinkling a magic dust over our food when we pray lends focus, and creates a ritual of something that we already know how to do. We are blessing our food and asking that it nourish our bodies.

We can also sprinkle people with our magic dust. It is a way to bless them and wish them well. We can do this in person or from afar. Magic has no boundaries or limitations of time and space.

When you sprinkle and bless another with magic dust, you are giving both you and the other person Joy. You are spreading Joy to the world. Of course, you could just do the same thing without any dust. The Power is in the blessing. The dust simply scatters it and extends the focus of the blessing. You could call the dust *joy dust*, and then when you sprinkle it on another person you would be sprinkling Joy on them.

When some magical occurrence happens and we see it, of course, we feel Joy.

In my first book *From Heartache to Joy*, I described an experience I had with a shopping cart.

## The Shopping Cart

It was early spring, 2014, and I was pulling into a parking space at a grocery store in Rockford, Illinois. The last traces of slush and snow were disappearing into the parking lot drains. I had escaped from my mom's house to do her grocery shopping. I needed a break from taking care of her. I was frustrated about being told what to do, when to do it, and how to do it.

I couldn't pull all the way into the parking space because a grocery cart was in the way. I couldn't back out because a car was pulling out behind me. I was stuck.

So I waited. Then I got fierce and waved my invisible magic wand at the cart. I yelled at it to move. "Move. Damn it!" It didn't move. *Great,* I thought. *My magic wand isn't working. Some person could move it for me.*

And right then a man walked by, grabbed the offending cart, and moved it out of the way. I was dumbfounded.

I quickly thanked the universe for answering my request, and gave a little chuckle.

We think the universe should respond in a certain way. It always responds—but it responds in its own way.

The universe does have my back. My magic wand is working. Silly me, being hung up on how.

We need to quit trying to determine how magic will show up and what it should look like. Magic has no boundaries. That is why it is called magic. We need only to enjoy it when it happens in our presence. The Joy of Magic is easy.

## Joy through Divine Perfection

*Divine Perfection*

Joy comes from realizing that everything is really in Divine Perfection. Joy comes from realizing that we can't do better or plan better than God or the Universe have already planned. We might think that we have a better plan and that our timing is better. But it isn't. We get to choose *what* we want but we don't get to decide *when* or *how* it happens. And even when we do choose *what,* the Universe is always asking us, *And how about now? What do you choose now?*

We have to keep on choosing. We never stop choosing. If we stop, then the Universe chooses for us. Then you might say, *Well, it knows better. So, what's wrong with that?* Well, the Universe thinks that you have chosen what you don't want, and gives you more of that. Not choosing is also choosing. So, you might as well choose what you do want.

*Conditional Happiness*

Conditional happiness occurs when you get what you want or asked for. Joy happens when you accept that the Universe has a plan, and you can join in that plan making choices to guide your boat downstream. When you accept Divine Perfection, then you quit struggling and you simply choose what would make you happiest or be the most fun. Then you discover that there is Joy in the world, and you will have some of that. Then you choose Joy. Because Joy is a choice. It is not a condition of something that has happened. Although that can also occur. But conditional Joy doesn't last. In fact, nothing lasts except the Love of God. And the Joy of God.

*The Dance*

Divine perfection is a dance. The Universe asks us to dance with it. And asks, *Will you dance with me here? And how about over here?* I say *yes. I will dance with you anywhere.* Having danced with the Universe in its dance of Divine Perfection, we begin to see the Joy in the dance. We can celebrate the Joy found in the dance of Divine Perfection.

## Joy through Purpose

*Focus*

We know when we are acting from our purpose or a purpose or maybe even God's purpose. We also know when we are on point. What if all those purposes and points were the same action? What if they were all pointed in the same direction? I would say sharpen your pencils! But nobody uses pencils anymore. So, what do we sharpen? We sharpen our awareness and our focus. Awareness is more spread out. Focus is sharp. But we need both. So, we spread out our awareness to a greater degree, a greater distance, and we narrow our focus down to our aligned purpose.

*Joy as a Tool*

We can use Joy to know that we are on the right path. If we are joyful, then this is the right path. This is not a conditional happiness kind of joy, like when you win the lotto. It is a kind of Joy that exudes from you when you are doing something that you love.

For me my path is Joy. And spreading Joy. If the path isn't Joyful, then it isn't the right path. I have asked the universe to sprinkle rose petals on my path so that it is easier for me to recognize it. The Universe obliges me and does, and then I can stop and smell the roses. Literally. If the path is sweet and smells of roses, I know it is the right path. Even if I am shoveling manure in the stable building. I love the smell of horse poop. Not exactly roses, but I love the smell anyway.

Ask the universe how you can recognize your path. The Universe will let you know. Or ask that it be shown to you in a certain way. Like a color. For example, if you see yellow, then that is the right path. If it is red, then that isn't the right path. Choose your own colors. And ask to be show those colors. Walking on your path of purpose will bring you Joy. When you feel Joy, you know that you are on the right path.

# Joy through Energy

*Joy Energy*

If we were to catch just one of the sparkles of Joy that the Universe continually rains down on us, we would erupt into such a glory that the whole world would be changed forever. From just one tiny sparkle.

> *Crying is a great way to release old baggage and heal old wounds. Laughing is a great way to make sure you don't spend too much time crying.*
>
> —Tom O'Keefe

*Laughter*

My Morning Prayer brought me to the word *laughter*. I let it go, and then I drew a card from my Morning Prayer Card deck, and it was *laughter*. So, okay. I'm stepping into Laughter today. I looked at the frog on the face of the card with the words, *Frog croaks swamp and gunk*. There are no frogs outside today. It is 9 degrees Fahrenheit and very cold. The frogs are sleeping. So, where do I get my laughter today? Everywhere.

I wrote about laughter in *Beyond Joy*, the second book in The Joy Series. I wrote how laughter changes the chemicals in our bodies. It releases cortisone and reduces blood pressure.

> **Laughter** *is fun, feels good, and keeps us from taking our lives too seriously. It keeps us in our hearts and helps us to let go of the judgement of our minds. It helps to release stress and keeps us in relaxation. A good belly laugh provides the health benefits of improved blood flow, lower levels of the stress hormone cortisol, and a more efficient immune system. Laughter is freeing because we let go of control. Laughter can deepen our relationship with ourselves and with others. When we laugh, we make a connection, to ourselves, to others, and to the universe. Laughter brings us to the present moment. God has a sense of humor. There is always a cosmic joke on the horizon. Can't you hear the frogs laughing? I do.*
>
> —*Beyond Joy*

*Laughter Bubbles Up*

When I came home from a Life Transformed coaches' reunion last week, I was so filled with Joy that laughter just kept bubbling out. The next morning John was talking, and he said the word, "canoe." I heard *Knu*. And I thought it was so funny, I laughed. A little bit later he said the words, "fishing lure." The word *lure* sound so funny. I couldn't stop laughing. Were the words inherently funny? No. Was he describing an incident that was funny? No. A joke is designed to be funny. It twists the conclusion around so that our minds end up upside down. Our minds find that funny. And then our bodies begin to laugh.

Laughing uncontrollably and ending up on the floor, we say LOL is so good for all of us. Our body, mind, and spirit are all laughing. And we are letting go of control. The energy of Joy makes the laughter bubbles rise up and out like the champagne bubbles in a glass.

*Make and Have Fun*

We say, "make fun of," and I use that phrase to describe laughter. We "make fun of" words, phrases, ideas, ourselves, and sometimes groups of people. We are the funniest when we make fun of ourselves. We aren't meant to take ourselves so seriously. We are meant to have fun, enjoy life, and laugh.

Today I intend to laugh at everything. I take a step. That's funny I say. And I laugh. Why? Because it feels good. I don't need any reason. I am making fun. The way a child makes fun.

Why did I choose frogs for the animals on the Laughter card? Because one night when John and I were fishing, we heard the frogs croaking in the lily pads. They were saying *Gunk* and *Swamp*. They croaked with very pronounced and extended words of the *swaaamp* and *guuunk* that they were sitting in. We thought it was hysterically funny and we laughed the rest of the night. And ever since when we hear frogs saying *swamp* and *gunk*, we laugh.

We have a gazebo outside our house and a pond with thousands of frogs. They croak all the time in the spring and the fall. They serenade the opposite sex. And still they say *swamp* and *gunk*. We laugh and they laugh with us. The more we laugh, the more they croak *swamp* and *gunk*.

They too are making fun of their lives, in their lives. As we should. So, with every step I take, I shall say, *Waaaaalk*, and when I sit down I shall say, *Siiiit*. And I shall laugh.

# Sacred Technologies of Absolute Joy

*Techniques for Joy through Peace*

1. **Dissolve Negative Energies**. Stand in the energy that is the opposite of the negative energy. If you are confronted with hate, stand in love; in fear, stand in courage; in struggle, stand in peace. Do not engage the other person in conflict. Allow them to have their feeling, until they don't. Say, *I'm sorry you hate that so. I know that must be painful. I don't hate it.*

*Techniques for Joy through Magic*

2. **Bless Your Food** with a sprinkle of magic dust. Also do this with coffee and water.
3. **Bless Other People** and your family with magic dust. Do it with or without them being aware of it. Wish them well and give them Joy. You can also bless strangers on the street.
4. **Bless Yourself** with magic dust. Sprinkle it on yourself. Give yourself Joy.

*Techniques for Joy through Divine Perfection*

5. **Energy of Joy.** Ask the universe to show you what Joy feels like.
6. **Energy of Divine Perfection.** Ask the universe to show you what Divine Perfection feels like.
7. **Joy through Divine Perfection.** Ask the universe to show you the Joy in Divine Perfection. What does that feel like?
8. **Accept Divine Perfection.** Say three times, *I* (state your name) *now accept the dance of Divine Perfection.*
9. **Dance Divine Perfection.** Say three times, *I* (state your name) *will now dance the dance of Divine Perfection with Joy.*

*Techniques for Joy through Purpose*

10. **Color of the Path**. Ask the universe to show you your right path by showing you a color.
11. **Recognition**. Ask the universe how you can recognize the correct path for your purpose.
12. **Joyful Path**. Ask if this path is bringing you Joy.
13. **Laugh** for no reason.

CHAPTER 3

# ABSOLUTE PEACE

 Absolute Peace is about absolute allowance.

## Peace of Peace

*Dream: Division*

> People seem to be divided into two groups. I am sitting on
> a bus reading a book when a division seems to occur. Those
> who read this book and those who don't. I don't understand
> the division. I share the book, and some of those around me
> who are my friends seem to believe. Others don't.
>
> Then the other group starts herding people up into
> groups. They live together, and they pull more people into
> their way of thinking and living. I live off with my friends.
> But one by one my friends disappear into the other group or
> are killed. One day the others show up at my door. I grab a
> kitchen knife to protect myself. I say, I will protect myself. But
> a man keeps coming. Then I make a small cut on his cheek
> to show him I am serious about protecting myself. He keeps
> coming. I wake up.

*Allowance*

I thought that the dream was strange. Then I asked myself, *Why have we divided ourselves into groups that feel the need either to kill others or to bring them into our way of thinking?* This started with reading a book. Why do we believe that only our way is the one true right way? Why do we feel right about the judgements we make? We need to wake up from this dream also. We need to live our lives in allowance. We need to allow others to believe differently than we do, and not try to convince them that our way is the right way or the only way.

> *People who want to share their religious view with you almost never want to you to share yours with them.*

> —DAVE BARRY.

## Peace through Joy

How can Joy bring us Peace? When we feel Joy, we are looking at the world through the rose-colored glasses of Joy. Our current joyful perception takes the edge off any struggle that we might be engaged in as well as the struggle we see around us. Peace is the absence of struggle. When the edge of struggle is taken off, we can step back and ask ourselves, *Do I really want to participate in this struggle? Is it even a real struggle? Does struggle exist?* It sure seems to exist. After all a lot of people seem to be doing it.

*Why Do We Struggle?*

Ask yourself, *Why am I doing this? If I want to continue doing this, is it really hard? Or is it interesting or maybe even exciting or fun?* So, then how did it go from being a struggle to being fun?

Then I ask myself, *Can I let my mind go to already done? Is it really already done? Then what am I doing? I am participating. I am going with the flow. Going with the flow is easy. I can choose to ride down the hill on my sled or I can climb up the mountain pulling my toboggan behind me.*

*Feeding the Horses.*

In order to feed the horses in the morning, I pull a toboggan loaded with a bale of hay. Then I do it again in two different directions for each of two herds with the grain. Twice for each herd. It is twenty degrees Fahrenheit outside. It can be a struggle in the deep snow. With clothes so thick that I can barely walk. It takes fifteen minutes to put all those clothes on and another fifteen minutes to take them all off.

In this process, I can choose to see myself struggling. Or I can choose for it to be easy. I could also choose it to be fun. Today it is cold and snowing. How do I choose to see it today? I choose to see it through fun and Joy. I don't try to get it done as fast as I can. But rather I stop looking down at my feet as I pull the toboggan, look up at the world, take a deep breath, and breathe in the Peace that I see around me. I look off into the distant woods. Up at the sky and back over at the house nestled in the banks of plowed snow. Hurry offers only a sense of struggle. Stopping offers the potential for Joy. It offers peace. And then all of a sudden, the job is done. I notice that it is already done. And I go into the house feeling not exhausted from the labor, but invigorated.

🌹 *You can't track the actions of people or of shadow governments while also tracking your own unlimited value.*

## Peace through Love

Peace is a color of Love. I have called it blue. Others may give it a different color. It isn't the color that is important. It is the fact that peace is one of the aspects and conditions of the Universe or God. Aspects are feelings. And Peace is certainly that. It is also a condition of our surroundings whether that is our community, country, or workplace. And even our household.

Love is the be all and end all answer to an unpeaceful situation. When we Love someone, it is impossible not to be at Peace with them and with ourselves. It starts with loving ourselves. And then we need to Love the other person, our family, the workplace, and the community.

But *I don't love this other horrible person,* you might say. It isn't the person that you hate. It is the situation that you hate. Separate the action from the person and Love the person. You don't have to like their behavior. When you Love the person, you will see it differently, and their behavior may eventually change. In the meantime, you are at Peace.

They can't be pulling on the other side of a rope that you have already let go of. The rope falls to the ground. And then what can the two of you pick up? A relationship based on mutual respect. This is true for all relationships.

## Peace through Abundance

When we recognize that the universe is infinitely abundant, then there is no reason to fight wars over trying to control the wealth in the world. There are distribution inequalities. Lasting peace would seem to require an equal distribution of the infinite wealth that is in the world. Maybe the distribution doesn't have to be equal. It just has to be enough for people to live their lives with dignity.

### Inherent Right to Live

All people have the inherent right to a life of ease and beauty. And all the other aspects that are the conditions and tools of our existence. But until food, clean air, and water are provided, the other aspects are not really important. Then perhaps the right to health is most important. Only then—when they are no longer concerned with survival—can people be concerned about their relationship with God or others. And only then can they be concerned with how they live their lives, with beauty, grace, and harmony. But until they can even live their life, they can't be concerned with those secondary aspects.

### An Opportunity

Abundance exists, and it affords the opportunity for Peace. A life without struggle. It is our duty as humans to feed and house the world. To stop the wars of greed and hoarding. To stop the wars that instill *a power over* and not a *power of.* Peace is a stronger power than *power over.* The power of Peace through the recognition of Abundance affords the most power. It is up to us as humans to redistribute that abundance so that all can live with adequate food and housing. Then we can all live in Peace.

# Peace through Health

## *A Confrontation*

When we aren't healthy, we are usually stressed. *Dis ease* is a kind of stress. Sometimes we go into struggle around our health. We say that we are struggling with … a cold. Fill in the blank with what kind of unwellness you are dealing with. By *dealing with*, I mean some kind of confrontation you are having with some aspect of your health. This is truly a confrontation you are having. It is not Peace.

All of this is the opposite of Peace. So, when we do none of it, when we stop confronting it, we are at Peace. We need to stop the war on disease. When we let go of war and confrontation, we can let go of struggle. When we let go of struggle, not only are we in Peace, but we also find ourselves in or headed toward wellness.

## *Wellness*

Wellness does bring Peace to our lives. If you want more peace, get more wellness. If you want more wellness, get more Peace. So, which comes first? Deal with wherever you are right now. If you are already at Peace, then bring that peace into every part of your body. If you are well but feel that you are struggling with some part of your life, then bring that absolute wellness into that part of your life where you are struggling. Ask yourself, *What does wellness feel like? What does health feel like?* Bring that feeling into the part of your life where you are struggling.

Ask yourself, *What does Peace feel like?* Bring that sense of ease and already done into your body. Bring it into the part of your body that is distressing you.

# Peace through Gratitude

*Breath*

From Dragon to Dragon Fly, the dragon breathes fire. He cleanses and there is a rebirth. The breath is a rebirthing tool. It also regulates our lives. And it gives us life. It calms us when we are anxious. We can do seven-second breathing. Breathe in for seven seconds and out for seven seconds. Do this five times. That calms and regulates our breathing.

When we regulate our breathing, we regulate our emotions. We slow everything down. We can change from anxiety to peace. With our breath, we can ease our struggle. We can pause and look at we what we are doing and then start again having let go of the need to struggle. And then we can simply perform the act we had been struggling with but without the struggle.

We can also cleanse our beliefs and past history with our breath. Conscious breathing as in a whole circular breath done for thirty minutes with a breath work coach can clean out any past limitations in the form of beliefs or emotions that we are hanging onto.

*Caring*

How does our breath relate to caring? Our breath brings us a state of peace. And from that place we can offer empathy. Caring is allowing another to experience the journey that they need to take in order to step forward. It is allowing ourselves to experience what we need to in order to step forward. Caring is about allowance. Allowance with kindness and encouragement.

We are kind because we are not harsh in our assessment and interaction with another. It is how we interact with another that is important. We act with kindness. We act with love. We act with complete allowance of everything that has gone on to date. That is where communication comes into the mix.

> *The single biggest problem in communication is that we believe that it has taken place.*
>
> —William H Whyte

*Communication*

When the other person asks us what we think about something, we could say, *I think you are doing a great job. To take the next step, you could ....* We don't say that they are wrong. We say that they are right and that the next right step might be this or that, and that the decision is theirs. We don't take over their decision making. To suggest what is right or wrong is disempowering. Allowance of their ability to make their own right decision is empowering.

Allowance with ourselves is trickier. We ask ourselves the question, *What should I do next?* I start with not only allowance but acceptance, then gratitude for it, and then a celebration of it because it has brought me to asking the question, *What should I do next?* It has brought me to this moment. When we let go of the judgment of everything that has occurred, we are able to step forward. The judgment keeps us mired down in the muck. Letting go of the judgement allows the muck to fall away. And it is much easier to move forward.

We hang on to the past because we believe that we are informed by it. What if we can be aware of it without judgment? Then with that awareness, we can decide to move forward. And we can decide how to move forward.

Isn't that just semantics, being informed by something and being aware of something? No. Being informed by our past has the result of our being held in place by what has gone before. It limits our ability to make new decisions. We believe that we can only do certain things. Having an awareness of a past event says that yes, we are aware of it, but it doesn't influence anything that we might do in the future or right now. Our past does not dictate or create our future. Only our present moment does. That is the difference. Don't let your past dictate this present moment. Be aware that it occurred, and then, now, make a decision to do whatever you think to do.

The dragon breathes fire and the dragonfly flickers and says, *I am a dragon too. I am a dragon too. Care about me.* Start with your breath. Find peace in awareness of your breath. Show allowance with kindness and encouragement. Be grateful for that other person and the experience he has brought into your life. Be grateful for the situation you are in because it has brought you to this point. Empower yourself with gratitude and you will discover that you are already in Peace.

## Peace through Magic

What if all of a sudden there was Peace? Wouldn't that be magical? You might ask, *But how can we make it happen?* We can't make magic happen. The whole point of magic is that we can't control it. *Yes, but,* I say.

We don't control it except that we encourage it when we believe in it. We believe in the Peace and we believe in Magic. We believe in the magic of peace. Peace is certainly a magical moment. And we believe that our belief can bring about what we believe in through the power of the focus of our intention. Where we place our attention and therefore our resulting intention and therefore our belief, grows.

The Universe joins with our focus. It brings about more of what we are focusing on. If that focus is war or struggle, then that is what we get more of. If it is Peace, then that is what we get more of. So, believe in Peace and focus on that. And know that magic or the force of the unexplainable Universe will bring it into being.

## Peace through Intention

*Peace*

There are so many waves we can ride on—Peace, Gratitude, and Joy. We recreate our own algorithm in every moment. Take a deep breath and choose Peace. We choose Peace by intending peace. By placing our attention there.

When we are feeling anger, how do we make a choice for Peace? We feel the anger and then we choose peace after the fact. Choosing after the fact is okay. So, make a choice then.

## *Dissipation of Energy*

When you are in pain or feeling any lower emotion, try this technique to dissipate the energy. Take seven steps forward. Turn around. Look at where you were standing. Dissipate the energy in the place where you were standing. Watch it dissipate. Wave your fingers at it and tell it to dissipate. Whatever we believe in works. It is our belief that is creating the dissipation of the energy.

 Like a temp agency, Life will put you to work.

## *Where Do You See Peace?*

Look around yourself and ask, *Where do I see Peace already in my life?* Make a list of where you already see Peace in your life. Write the list down. Do this for one week. Then ask yourself if you notice more Peace in your life. Remember that what you focus on is what you get. So, the act of noticing Peace brings you more Peace.

I ask myself, *Where do I see Peace?*

- In the gentle flames of the fire.
- In the ticktock of the clock.
- In my breath as I write.
- In the sips of coffee from my pink cup.
- In the reviewing and numbering of what I have written.
- In John sitting and moving things around on his phone.
- In the quiet of the room.
- In the gentle falling of the snow outside.
- The light dusting that is on the ground.
- In the dove that picks at the seeds under the feeder.

The more we notice that all things can bring us Peace, the more Peace we will feel. It is the action of the noticing that leads to our attention. And our attention will remind us that what we notice, we intend. Why not intend Peace?

*Tradition is the illusion of permanence.*

—WOODY ALLEN

# Peace through Divine Perfection

*Relationship to Self*

I was thinking about my relationship to my job. I currently run The Joy Project. I've written a few books and created a few courses. I'm grateful for what is. But does that constitute a business? My tax accountant says it does. If I spend eight hours a day working on it. Currently I do that. I'm grateful for what I am already doing. I think I should do more. By that I mean reach more people. Sell more books. Teach more classes or speak more often. It is not that I want to spend more time. But that I want to reach more people. I know that to change the world, I have to be the change that I want to see. I also know that the world is already changed. But I don't quite see it.

There is a lot of talk about passive income. The dictionary defines passive income as "income that requires little to no effort to earn and maintain. It is called progressive passive income when the earner expends little effort to grow the income." That's great. I like the little effort part, but somehow, I link that to passive people.

People relate to the actions we are taking. The emotions and energy we put into our products. Our products are a sharing of ourselves. We have a relationship with our customers. Matt Kahn recently released meditation cards. I released my cards a few weeks ago. He says that his cards are "energetically encoded." I believe that all works of art are energetically encoded. But encoded with what?

*Energy Encoding*

Words and pictures carry energy. Fiction and story carry energy. Story carries us to another place where we experience what is being told. Giver and receiver. That is what is going on. The creator is the giver. The buyer is the receiver. I am grateful for all of the receivers who have experienced my books, classes, and presentations. I will continue to give the energy of Joy.

The world is polarized, and the energy is speeding up. All is as it should be. I offer one way to slow down, smell the roses, and experience the Joy that is the gift of life. It's December. This time of the year is particularly fast. Lots of holiday parties and visiting family and friends. There's a lot of hustle and bustle. With the new year there is also some thought given to change. A change in our lives. Presumably for the better.

*A New Year's Resolution*

What if the only change we need to make is to be grateful for what is? Then what happens is a change is made. It is our relationship with ourselves that needs to change. We just need to accept who we already are. It's the easiest change, the change of no change. And then we see change.

*Tap Your Forehead*

We need to trust in the work we are doing and surrender to the life we are already living. Trust in your work. Ride the wave of your breath. Surrender and trust. Tap on your forehead like a Southern Baptist. Allow the Grace to take over. A blessing is being touched by the power of Grace. Allow the Grace of Dive Perfection to bring you Peace.

## Peace through Purpose

How can we achieve peace through Purpose? If "Our purpose is to discover our purpose" as the fortune cookie says, then we are always in the state of discovering. That is true. We are always in the state of discovering. I am in the state of Joy. Always discovering more Joy and how to spread Joy. That is my Purpose. And I am always in the state of rediscovering how to do and be that Joy.

Sometimes it is fun and laughter that I spread. How is that peaceful? I also seem to be at Peace when I am spreading fun and laughter. When I am writing about it in one of my books. There is the absence of struggling.

There is the absence of war or confrontation. I can only call it peaceful. And I call it joyful at the same time. It is Peace through Joy, or through Purpose, my Purpose.

## Peace Energy

Peace is calm, quiet. It is blue. Does it have a taste? I think that maybe it tastes like blueberries. It is easy. It is already done. It is without struggle. It is without hard work. But it does contain participation. We participate with ease. We go with the flow. There is a pause. We take a deep breath. We exhale. We are at Peace.

How can we be at Peace in the midst of chaos? We pause. We don't join in the fray. Instead we stand back and then we act from our own Peace of mind. We participate from that place. We make better choices and decisions from that place, from the energy of Peace.

## Sacred Technologies of Absolute Peace

*Techniques for Feeling Peace through Joy*

1. **Let Go of Struggling**. Let go of struggling with whatever you are doing. Stop. Take a few deep breaths. Look around you. Be grateful for being here. Choose to participate in what you are doing from *That's interesting*. Or *That's fun* or *That's ...* fill in the blanks with something other than struggle.
2. **Choice.** Say three times, *I choose to let go of the idea of struggle. I choose easy. I choose fun. I choose ....*
3. **How Easy?** Ask three times, *I wonder how easy this could possibly be?* Then wait and watch.

*Technique for Peace through Love*

4. **Love Anyway.** When you are in a situation where you don't agree with a person's action, separate their behavior from the person. You

don't have to like their actions. But you have to like the person. Love them anyway.

## *Techniques for Peace through Health*

5. **Glowing Health.** Ask yourself, *What does wellness feel like? What does health feel like?* Bring that feeling into the part of your life that is struggling. See health as glowing and vigorous. Then bring glowing and vigorous into your wealth or your relationship. Bring it where you need it. Bring it to wherever you struggle.
6. **Cell Ease.** Ask yourself what does Peace feel like? Bring that sense of ease and already done into your body. Bring it into the part of your body that is distressing you. Bring it into every cell of your body.

## *Techniques for Peace through Gratitude*

7. **Seven Seconds Breathing.** Breathe in for seven seconds and out for seven seconds. Do this five times. This will calm you.
8. **Let go of Belief.** Let go of the belief that you are controlled by your past. Say three times. *By the law of divine grace and all that is light, I* (state your name) *let go of the belief that my past controls my present. I am here now.*
9. **Grateful.** Say three times, *By the law of divine grace and all that is light, I* (state your name) *am grateful for the situation I am in right now. Thank you. Thank you. Thank you.*

## *Techniques for Peace through Intention*

10. **Dissipate the Energy.** Take seven steps forward. Turn around. Look at where you were standing. Dissipate the energy where you were standing. Watch it dissipate. Wave your fingers at it and tell it to dissipate.
11. **Existing Peace.** Make a list of where you already see Peace in your life. Write the list down. Do this every day for one week.

*Techniques for Peace through Divine Perfection*

12. **Encode with Peace.** Say three times, *I now know that all products are encoded with energy. I choose those products that are encoded with Peace.*

13. **Accept No Change**. Say three times, *I accept who I already am. I accept the change of no change.*

14. **Tapping**. Say three times as you tap your forehead, *I tap my forehead with the blessing of Divine Perfection.*

*Techniques for Peace through Energy*

15. **Peace Energy.** Ask to be shown what the energy of Peace feels like. What color is it? What does it smell or taste like?

# CHAPTER 4

# ABSOLUTE LOVE

*Between what is said and not meant and what is meant and not said, most of love is lost.*

—KAHLIL GIBRAN

## Love of Love

*Dream: Flying and Going through the Wall*

*I am in a class with Rikka Zimmerman. She just finished talking and the group is getting ready to lie down on the floor. We have mats and are putting our heads toward the center of the room. Rikka leaves to make some arrangements. I roll over on to my stomach and decide to do a yoga plank. Then I think that my feet are very light, and from the plank position I let them go up into the air. I think that I could just levitate. I feel a little sticky. Then my feet go up and then all of me goes up. And I am floating. Then I am flying. I zoom around the room. I can bank right and I can bank left. I feel so free.*

*The people in the room watch me. They are amazed. Rikka comes back, and she laughs as if to say, "It's about time." She is happy.*

*Linda, a person on the other side of the room, is talking. Linda says. "I want to fly too. Why does she get to fly?" I just*

42

*shake my head. It isn't her thing, or she isn't ready to fly. I don't ask, "Why me?" Of course, I am flying.*

*Rikka asks, "What else can you do? Can you take it even further?" I wonder why she is pushing me. I land and walk over to a wall. I put my finger through it. She says, "Go further." I put my whole arm through it. She says, "Go further." I rip open a hole in the wall and I stick my head through it. Someone in the group says, "Just dematerialize and go through it."*

*I stick the upper part of my body through the wall and take a peek. Then I step through it. I look around. I don't see anything different. I see another wall, a log wall, and then I think now that's a wall and I stick my head through that thick wall. I feel all the wood around me.*

*Then I find myself in a place where I am being chased by an evil person. I am skipping across the roofs of buildings like those young people who can hop from building to building. But I am really jumping and flying if I need to. The evil person is still chasing me. I see the roof of a building. I think that if I go through this stadium type roof, I will get out of this place. But I think that there is a huge void between the bottom of the roof and the top of it. I don't want to go into that void.*

*He is still chasing me. He knows that I can fly but he doesn't know that I can go through walls. I think that I will get to the end of these roofs and go through the gate.*

*I turn around and he is right in front of me. He reaches up through my vagina and pulls out a package from my womb. It looks like the kind of packet that you pull out of a turkey. Full of giblets. I wonder what is in the packet and what it is for. I wonder if I will miss it. Then I turn to go for the gate. I wake up.*

*What Does It Mean?*

What does this dream mean? I have long ago determined that the evil person chasing me in my dreams is my own fear. I am running from my

43

own fear. When I stop to face it. I am not really facing it. It is simply there. The fear rips something out of my womb. What is that? It is the fear of limitation. The only thing limiting me is my own fear. As I step through the gate, I am entering this world with a new vision. I know what I lost. What is lost is the fear of limitation. When we face it and let it go, we can fly. It has taken me years to face and let go of that fear.

Our purpose is to live our lives fully. To experience. To do that we need to let go of fear. It is fear that keeps us in a box. Although that too is an experience. We let go of it by feeling it fully. And then we let it go. What is left is Love.

Love is all that is, and everything is simply a condition, aspect, tool, and a color of love. Absolute Love is love loving love.

 *Much more unites us as humans than divides us.*

## Human Love

This morning's meditation word was Love. *Okay,* I said. *So God, show me how much love I could be.* Almost instantly I started to cry. The tears were gentle tears. I thought about the love of a puppy or a kitten or a baby. The gentle love of a young couple when they first meet or the refined feeling like the fine wine of older love. Like the love I have for my husband of fifty-plus years. I wondered what that fine wine would taste like and I thought of the touch of my beloved's lips. That would be what it would taste like even though I have never had such a wine.

## The Diamond in Our Hearts

I thought about a person shining out the light of God from the center of their being. And what that would look like. It would look like the sun shining out. I thought that the light would have to pour into a being before it could go out. But from what direction? It would have to pour in from all directions, and in fact that is what it does. It pours in from all directions like it's going into a black hole in space. But where does it go? How does it reflect back out?

The light goes into the center of our being. And it reflects back out. It does so because at the center there is a diamond. Not a black hole. So, what is at the heart of God? It is emptiness. It is where nothing resides, but infinite possibilities surround it. All colors and smells and tastes. All the feelings that we can feel because we have bodies and senses to experience all possibilities.

## The Color of Love

Love has no color. But I would call the human kind of love red. All twenty-nine of the current aspects of God that I meditate on and write about have colors. But God's Love does not. It contains all things, and that color is black, but not really dark and not really grey and not really a mist. It is not really anything. It just is.

So, I shine out from the center. I am aware of God's Love. God Loves us even if we aren't aware of it. But when we are aware, we become it. We already are it, but now we are aware of already being it. And then we shine forth. Because there is a diamond inside each of our hearts or our center that reflects the light out. Are we the center? Yes and no. We are co-creators of that light through our awareness, acceptance, and celebration. We no longer hide our light under the cover of *I don't know* and *I am not aware*. We simply allow ourselves to shine forth what already is shining forth and then we celebrate it. Having celebrated it, we return to our awareness and acceptance to start the continuous process over again.

May you all shine your light forth from this moment forward. When we shine our lights together, how bright the future will be! Happy New Year! And guess what? It is always a happy new year.

 Tell everyone else: This is the value you bring to me.

# Love through Joy

## *Unconditional Love*

We usually think of human love as a kind of relationship. The relationship we have with our partner or friends and family members or with God. More often than not, it is a conditional relationship. If you love me, I will love you back. If I love you, perhaps you will love me. And the human kind of love is also seen in the love of a mother for her children and the love we give to a kitten or a puppy. It is in those practices that we are at our best in giving love. It is unconditional. And that is closer to the kind of Love that God gives us, which is totally unconditional.

True love is unconditional and by my definition is all that is. Love is all there is. By this I mean that Love contains all things.

## *The Color of Joy*

Joy is a color of all the things Love contains. It is but one color in a rainbow of colors that turns into a whiteness with no definition. Joy is a separation from that whiteness. It is a feeling and an action. In humanity there is a kind of giving and receiving involved. Although there is really no giving or receiving. There is just an exuding while other people stand in the presence of that Joy and they are infected with it. Almost like a virus. It is the virus of Joy. And it is infectious.

Love might be considered infectious also, but because that is all there is, there is no place for it to go. So, a slightly more defined energy is put out there. That is the energy of Joy. Although the human kind of relationship of love is also a lesser energy than the all-inclusive Love energy. So, the human form of love energy as we know it can be shared also.

Joy is happy, moving, and exuding. It brings us closer to Love because it is something that we can define as well as give and receive. Or at least exude. So, Love is increased with our active pursuance of and being in Joy.

 The Universe brings unlimited value everywhere.

# Love through Abundance

God gives us his love through an abundant Universe. Or the Universe gives us the infinite abundance of itself. There can be no beginning and no end because it is infinite. There is no lack. There is only a difference in distribution. It is up to us how that abundance is distributed. The current politics of the United States are mired or maybe outlined by the distribution of education, healthcare, and the stewardship of our planet. I start with *mired* but change to *outlined* because it doesn't have to be muck and mire. It can be a platform for a benevolent future. That future is about how we distribute and share the abundance that is.

If we love, we don't hold onto things with greed or fear that there won't be enough. We share with our fellow man. We treat all others as if they were guests in our house. For some people, that means feeding them on our best china and giving them the best of our food. It is never in our own best interest to send them home and then feed our own family.

I am reminded of the story of "Stone Soup," in which an old woman boils a pot of water and puts in a rock. She tells her neighbors that she is making soup and invites them to come and share it with her. One by one they show up, each bringing a contribution to the soup. One has a carrot, another has an onion, and another has salt. One even has a small piece of dried meat. When it comes time to eat the soup, each person receives a delicious bowl of warm, invigorating soup.

# Love through Health

*Total Allowance*

Since Love is total allowance and acceptance of what is, then that means that to stand in Love, we also have to accept our current state of wellbeing or health. The novel coronavirus is running rampant in the world as I write this. There is a lot of fear in the world. The stock markets have crashed for days. So, even our economy is reacting to the fear. The fear of not being well. I made a grocery list yesterday for my husband to get groceries for two weeks so that we would be prepared for a two-week period of staying at home. Is that fear or just being prepared? Caution is not really fear. I am feeling cautionary. And I allow that feeling.

## The Absence of Fear

So, what does Love have to do with it? Love is the absence of fear. And it is allowing the feelings that we are having. Not denying them. Until we don't feel them. Then we can move on into accessing the Love that is already inside of us and waiting to come out.

Of course, when we are unhealthy, we are down and in bed or maybe just compromised in some way. Perhaps we have a broken leg. Or maybe we are suffering from a disease. Any of those things can keep us from having a relationship with another whether we are physically indisposed or maybe we just don't feel like relating. When we have robust energy, we are much more likely to interact with another person. When I am sick, I just want to be left alone and go to bed.

My husband wants people to wait on him. And take care of him. He has a different approach. But then he is an extrovert and I am an introvert. Although my mother was an extrovert and she wanted to be left alone when she was sick. So maybe extroversion and introversion have nothing to do with it. Maybe it's just learned behavior.

## Wellness

I think that wellness is about loving ourselves. It's hard to Love ourselves when we are sick. We are usually in judgment about how we have done something wrong; or we wouldn't be sick in the first place. What if being sick has nothing to do with doing something wrong? It just is.

We need to accept that it is and move on to getting well. If we can Love our current state of health for what it is, then we can move on to being healthier.

I had a touch of the flu a couple of weeks ago. I almost never get sick. I wondered why I was sick. But then I just said, *Oh well, I'm going to bed until I feel like I can get up.* And I did. I was dizzy, tired, and didn't feel like doing anything. There were a few moments when I enjoyed being on the couch doing nothing. I did judge myself, saying that I had been working too hard without a break. I needed to just stop everything. And I did. My body was telling me to stop. Did I do something wrong? I let myself go into judgement for just a short time. Then I let it go. Not stopping might have been wrong; but the virus stopping me was definitely right. So, did I Love the flu? Not exactly. But I did like the stopping very much.

### *Love Your Body*

We don't have to love our colds. But we should love our bodies for their right reactions to our behavior. We should love our bodies for their ability to adapt and heal themselves.

We should be grateful for the miracle and magic that our bodies are. They can for the most part heal themselves. There are times when we need to assist them with medicine and rest or a different behavior. But that's okay. We are in a relationship with our bodies. And that relationship is a loving relationship. Each of us has a body that is grateful to us for all the assistance we give it. And we are grateful to our bodies for all the experiences they give us. After all, without our bodies we would have awareness but no experiences.

 Arrogance is a comparison.

## Love through Gratitude

### *Gratitude Is Conditional*

Gratitude is a catalyst for many things. Of course, it is a catalyst for love. When you say, *I am so grateful for you* or *for this thing happening*, what are you really saying? With a person you are also saying, *I love you*. With an event, it isn't so obvious. But it is the same. So, gratitude and love are very closely related. Gratitude is usually conditioned on something. Something happens and we are grateful for it. Love doesn't work that way. Love is unconditional. If what we feel is conditional, it is gratitude and not love.

Although we feel some love primed by the gratitude pump, it is still conditional. It is conditioned on whatever happened. Love is unconditional.

We don't love someone because they have blue eyes or are beautiful. We love their blue eyes and we love their beauty. We are grateful that they have blue eyes and we are grateful that they are beautiful. Our love for them is independent of their blue eyes and their beauty.

*Universal Love*

God or the Universe loves us no matter what. *No matter what* is the definition of Love. We are forgiven our trespasses. If fact, *forgiven* doesn't exist. Because there is nothing to forgive. God accepts us the way we are with all our faults, and loves us anyway. We are always perfect just the way we are. He doesn't care whether we have blue eyes or brown eyes. He doesn't care whether we are beautiful or ugly. In his eyes we are all beautiful. So how does he decide which one is the most beautiful? Always the next one he looks at is the most beautiful.

Do you want to have more Love in your life? Be grateful for the love that is already in your life. Say thank you, God, for the beautiful partner I have in my life. Then he or she will seem even more beautiful than they were just a moment ago. Be grateful for the friends you already have, and you will have even more friends. Be grateful for the family you already have, and you just might find that you like them even more. Be grateful for the life you have, and you will find that tomorrow you will like your life even more. Love in all your relationships starts with gratitude for what you already have.

## Love through Magic

Love is magical. The human kind of love puts us in a very magical state. We are full of Joy and optimism. We see the world through rose-colored glasses. And true Love, the Love of the Universe, contains all things. So, magic is an aspect of Love. Magic is a kind of separation from the Universe so that it can create and know itself through the expression of Magic. Something doesn't exist. And then it does. How much fun it that!

Love is total acceptance and total allowance of all things. And all things already exist and have the potential to exist. Out of that potentiality something appears. We call that Magic. Magic is simply the Universe creating in front of us. And by our observing it, together we observe it. And then it exists. That is Magic. We allow it and we accept it. And so does the Universe. We say, *Yes. And what else is there?* The Universe says, *Yes. And what else is there?*

## Love through Intention

### The Light Switch

I began studying with Rikka Zimmerman many years ago in 2010. I heard her on a couple of webinars, both Jennifer McClean's and Darius Barazandeh's. What caught my attention at those times was when I heard her say, "All you have to do is say *Yes*. It's that simple." She used the analogy of flipping a light switch. I thought, *Hmmm. Flipping a light switch. Now that's easy. And I like easy.* So, I took a live class with her in Chicago, and that began a long apprenticeship into life coaching.

What I didn't realize at the time was that you have to keep flipping the light switch in every moment. You can't just flip it once and expect it to stay there. I've been in many classes where people complain, *Why can't I feel as good when I go home as I feel here when I am in class?*

The problem is that when you go home you are present with the trials and tribulations of life. And when you are in class you are present for the love that is in class and are generally in the present moment. Of course, you feel good in the presence of love. So how do you bring the present moment of love back home into the trials of your life?

### The Rheostat Switch

The universe doesn't understand *no*. It only hears the vibration of *Yes*. So today I thought about that, and I came up with the vision of a rheostat switch. You just turn on the *Yes* and leave it there. That is even easier than continuing to flip the switch on *Yes*. What's also great is that you can turn up the intensity of yes. More intensity of yes and the stronger your energy is in receiving whatever wonderful thing the universe is waiting to share with you.

*Yes* puts you in the eternal flow. You are going with the flow instead of against it. Even when you believe your answer is no, look for something to say *Yes* about, and put your attention there. All creation is the energy of yes. There is no *No. No* is a nono. HA! Now that's funny.

## Love through Presence

*Snowfall*

This morning during my meditation I looked out across the snow and thought, *WOW. This is gorgeous.* Five inches of new snow fell during the night and piled up on the branches of the trees.

And the wind had not yet blown it off. Everything was covered in a new blanket of white, which seemed to join everything together. The new snow had unified everything. It unified the huge piles of plowed snow with the new fallen snow on the driveway. Then I wondered how I would get through the deep snow to feed the horses this morning. From present moment *Wow* to worry. How does this happen? *Oops,* out of the present moment. That is how it happens.

*Past, Present, and Future*

Love is the embracing of the everlasting now. How do I get to that? First, I take a look at the past. The past informs what we are currently doing and tries to inform what we will do in the future. The present informs our future. So, in that regard the past informs the present, which informs the future. Our mind uses the past to inform the present to keep us safe. That is the job of the mind. But in this moment, we are safe. So now what?

We live in the present moment. We look around us, we experience what is around us, and we move on to the next present moment. That is how being in the present moment works.

*Worry*

There is no fear in this moment unless we are looking into the future and worrying. That worry is conditioned on the past moment informing us about something that happened, something that we should be concerned about, to keep us safe. But that is also a limitation. Expecting the present or the future to react in a certain way based on the past is a limitation.

What if the future could be different? Remember, what we focus on is what we experience. And what if something wonderful happens because of the past? No. It isn't because of the past—it is because we are allowing it in the present moment.

*Marriage and Friendship*

Love is about total allowance. It is loving someone or something no matter what. We may not love their behavior, but we love them. We accept the behavior of our friends. We love them anyway.

Yesterday my husband of fifty-plus years went to a doctor's appointment; he was feeling sick. He shouldn't have gone, in my opinion. And it was going to snow in the afternoon. We live in the country forty-five minutes from Green Bay, WI. Of course, knowing him, I thought he should be home around 4:00 p.m. or 4:30 p.m. He is always late. At 5:00 p.m. and then 6:00 p.m. I became worried, and I thought he might have been in an accident. After all he was really sick. At a little after 6:00 p.m. he texts and says that he is at Costco doing some shopping. I get mad. I know that I shouldn't worry. I tell myself to just keep busy. I do, and I forget about him. He shows up around 7:30 p.m. He's fine, still a little sick. But I worried for nothing! Why do I do that?

Some people would say. Well, that's justified. It isn't about justification. Worry can make a person sick and serves no purpose. Worry sends us looking at a future that doesn't exist. When I am happiest, I am in the present moment. Worry takes us out of the present moment. Worry takes us out of happiness.

The past informing us of the present moment (or the worry in the present moment) is trying to take us into the future moment. So, I might be on my way to making myself sick by worrying. So I don't. I let it go.

*Love Who You Are*

Love lets it all go. You might think that Loving someone is worrying about him or her. It isn't. We can share what we think about something with them. But then we have to let them live their own life. If we can't stay in our own present moment with this, then we have a choice—we can let them know and forget about it. Or we can try to change them, which isn't love. Or we can forget about it and be in the present moment. Or we can leave.

Struggling with another person's behavior never works. Love them and yourself for who they and who you are. And guess what? Sometimes when we love them for who they are, they change. Sometimes they change in a way that we would like them to, and sometimes they change when we already think they are perfect the way they are. Change is also inevitable. Stay in the present moment.

How do I stay married to a man for fifty-plus years? I stay in the present moment. And when I forget and slide into worry, I bring myself back to the present moment. Love is about letting go of fear. We can let go of fear by feeling it until we don't feel it anymore. Then we can let it go. When we let the fear go, what remains is Love.

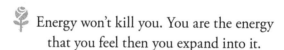 Energy won't kill you. You are the energy
that you feel then you expand into it.

## Love through Energy

*The Energy Volleyball.*

I've played imaginary volleyball with people before. Hitting the ball back and forth with all the histrionics of a real volleyball game. Reaching hard to get it, and jumping up high when necessary. It can be a lot of fun. This morning in my meditation, I decided to play with a group of people from a stage. I was presenting a lecture on energy sharing. The vehicle I chose to use was the volleyball.

*Volleyball Journey*

> *First, I create a volleyball in my hand, and I show it to the group. They smile. Some believe they see it, and some don't. I serve the volleyball out into the audience. And one person hits it back. I hit it back to the audience. We go back and forth a few times as if we are playing volleyball.*
>
> *Then I decide to share our hearts in the volleyball. I zip open up the front of my body, and take out energy from my heart and place it in the volleyball. Then I zip open the collective heart of the audience and place the energy from their heart into the volleyball. I hold up the volleyball to show them what we have created. It is a magnificent, glowing volleyball. I serve the newly made volleyball out into the audience. We hit the volleyball back and forth. A few times. I serve it up into the air and it explodes into a hundred volleyballs. There is one for each person. And then we go back and forth. The audience hitting a hundred balls and me sending them back.*
>
> *All the balls come at me, and I stop them in midair like Neo from the* Matrix Trilogy *did when he stopped the bullets. I pick up one of the volleyballs and look at it. I think to multi locate so that I am in front of each person and we share the energy of each volleyball between us.*
>
> *I stand back on stage, and I call all of my selves back to me and we play group volleyball one on a hundred. Back and forth, a hundred volleyballs all going into the air at the same time. Then I toss all the volleyballs into the air, and they come down in a million sparkles of light. I bask in the light of our sharing and love.*

What had we done? We shared the love of our hearts. We put it in a ball of light and played together. Play energetic volleyball with someone. Put the love of your heart into the volleyball, and pass it back and forth.

# Sacred Technologies of Absolute love

*Techniques for Love through Health*

1.  **Thank Your Body.** When your body seems to get well on its own or with your help, say, *Thank you, body, for healing yourself.* Say, *Thank you. Thank you. Thank you.*
2.  **Behavioral Awareness.** When you get sick and it seems to be the result of some behavior, say, *Thank you, body, for making me aware of my behavior. I will do better next time. I will take better care of you next time. Thank you. Thank you. Thank you.*

*Techniques for Love through Gratitude.*

3.  **Gratitude for Your Partner.** Say three times, *Thank you for the wonderful partner I have. Thank you. Thank you. Thank you.*
4.  **Gratitude for Your Friend.** Say three times, *Thank you for my best friend, …* (fill in the blank.) *Thank you. Thank you. Thank you.*
5.  **Gratitude for Your Family Members.** Say three times. *Thank you for my loving family.* (Say this even if they haven't been so loving in the past.) *Thank you. Thank you. Thank you.*
6.  **Gratitude for Life.** Say three times, *Thank you for the wonderful life I have. Thank you. Thank you. Thank you.*

*Technique for Love through Magic*

7.  **What Else?** Think about a situation or relationship that you would like to add some love to. Ask, *What else might I know about this? What else is there?* Listen.

*Techniques for Love through Intention*

8.  **Rheostat.** Create a rheostat for *yes.* Turn it on, and turn up the intensity. You can also turn it down when you don't need as much energy. Keep your *yes* running on low.

*Techniques for Love through Presence*

9. **Presence.** When you find yourself going into worry or anxiety, come back to the present moment. Remember the future does not exist. Only the present moment exists.

*Techniques for Love through Energy*

10. **Volleyball.** Play energetic volleyball with someone. Put the love of your heart into it, and pass it back and forth.

# CHAPTER 5

# ABSOLUTE ABUNDANCE

 *Abundance is the recognition of value.*

## Abundance of Wealth

*One day a young boy asked his father, "What is the value of my life?" Instead of answering, the father told his son, "Take this rock and sell it at the market. If anybody asks the price, raise two fingers and don't say anything," instructed the father.*

*The boy went to the market and sat down to wait. After a time, a woman asked, "How much is this rock? I would like to put it in my garden." The boy didn't say anything but raised up his two fingers, and the woman said, "Two dollars? I will take it." The boy did not sell her the rock. Instead the boy went home and told his father, "A woman wants to buy this rock for two dollars."*

*Then the father said, "Son, I want you to take this rock to a museum. If anybody wants to buy it, don't say a word, just put up your two fingers."*

*The next day the boy went to the museum. He sat on a bench and waited. After a while, a man showed up. The man said he would like to buy the rock. The boy didn't say a word but put up two fingers. The man said "Two hundred dollars? I will take it."*

*The boy was shocked. He did not sell the rock. Instead the boy went running home and told his father, "A man wants to buy this rock for two hundred dollars."*

*His father then said, "Son, the last place I want you to take this rock is to a precious stone store. Show it to the owner and don't say a word, and if he asks the price, just raise up your two fingers."*

*The next day the boy went to a precious stone store and showed the rock to the owner. "Where did you find this stone? It is one of the rarest stones in the world. I must have it! How much would you sell it for?"*

*The boy put up his two fingers, and the man said, "I will take it for two hundred thousand dollars." The boy did not know what to say. He did not sell the rock. Instead he returned home with the rock to his father. The boy told him, "There's a man who wants to buy the stone for two hundred thousand dollars.*

*His father then asked the boy, "Son, do you know the value of your life now?"*

I chose to start the chapter on abundance with this story which was originally told by Sean Buranahiran. It was retold several times on the internet. And I am retelling it here. How we feel about ourselves and the places where we put ourselves determine how wealthy we become.

*It matters where you decide to place yourself.*

—SEAN BURANAHIRAN

The place where we reside both physically and mentally determines our perception of Abundance. Our perception describes the conditions that surrounds us while at the same time co-creating those conditions. The abundance of wealth or more precisely the abundance of abundance is about the purity of the energy of abundance. I call this pure energy of abundance *Absolute Abundance*. This is the perception of Abundance as seen by Source. It is a reflection of the Abundance of the Universe and all that is.

# Abundance through Peace

*Freedom*

"Freedom is just another word for nothing left to lose." That's a line out of the song, "Bobby Magee." I think about the country and western interpretation of that, and of the howling pain that is in those songs, even though "Bobby Magee" isn't a country song. It's a folk song. In country songs, "Lost love" is usual and so is "he done me wrong." Freedom is about letting go of the fear of losing. Losing health and losing our wealth if we are wealthy. Losing our lover our relationship or our friends. Fear is about loss.

But what if we don't have to fear the loss of those things? What if we could get them back in the next moment? Maybe not the loss of a loved one. But do we really lose them to begin with? They have departed. But in a way they are always with us.

*The Golden Parachute*

The fear of loss shackles us to whatever is. If life is good, then it's a golden parachute that keeps us in a job that we don't really want but is too good or safe to let go of. If life is a struggle, then it is easier to let go, but we fear that what might be will be even worse than what already is. So, we hang on to what is. Even if we don't like it.

Yet, we can never really hang on. We are dragged down the river clutching to whatever is sticking out because we believe that the river is trying to drown us. The river is simply moving us downstream, however. We might as well go with the flow and end the struggle.

*Limitation of Virtues*

Freedom is not hanging on. To anything. Then there really is nothing left to lose. But then you might ask, *What about my values? Might I not be a bad person if I give up my values?* Values can only expand us to a certain point. And then they become limitations. The virtues can be seen as values and can be hard to let go of. The negative values such as greed and vanity are much easier to let go of. Although it seems that in this world greed is a very hard value to let go of. The greed and corruption that have caused our earth's current plight with climate change are rampant. Ignorance is also at play. As well as the blindness in the refusal to see what greed and corruption are causing on the planet.

These values or what many would call *a lack of values* are lessons. The planet has given us many warnings—the fires in California and Australia, and the flooding all over the world, including here in my tiny town of Algoma, Wisconsin. We need to heed the lessons and warnings before we destroy the future of this planet for our children. Greed is an addiction, and, like any addiction, it is hard to get rid of. The virtues and our addictions are the last to go. Freedom comes from letting them go.

*Letting Go*

How do we let go of our virtues and addictions? We could allow ourselves to bottom out. But that might take the planet with us. Or the planet might react in more violent ways until we take action to change our behavior. Or we could simply value Freedom more than our greed or our other addictive behaviors and our subtle values of what we call the virtues, like caring, giving, helping, and being spiritual, whatever that means.

I choose freedom. Absolute freedom. Above all else, above what many others call *spiritual*. Above my own addictions of wanting more and more. Of wanting to be spiritual or more caring or loving. By *loving* here, I mean in the human sense of *If you love me, I will love you back*. This is conditional love. No, I will love all, even if they don't love me and even if they persecute me. And I turn the golden rule around. *I will love myself as much as I love others*. Most of us have a hard time loving ourselves. The greed and corruption are happening because we are not truly *Loving* ourselves even though some might call that egotistical. Egotism happens because people are in fear. Fear of losing something. Not because they love themselves.

Freedom is stepping outside that fear and letting go of hanging on to whatever we are afraid of losing. I choose letting go and Freedom. Absolute freedom. There is nothing to lose because I have already let go of hanging on. That doesn't mean it is gone. It is just that I am not clinging to it. It can be there or not be there.

We have Peace when we don't care if something is or is not there. Abundance shows up when we don't care whether it is there or not. That is Abundance through Peace.

 True wealth is the wealth that we share with the world.

## Abundance through love

This morning, I drew the Morning Prayer cards of Abundance, Love, and Breath. I know that Love is all there is, and that Abundance is a color or aspect of Love. So, when we are not in the energy of Abundance, we are also not accepting the energy of Love. God and the Universe are abundant in all things. By definition, the Universe is abundant. It might not seem that way from where we are standing because we aren't choosing to perceive it that way.

We tend to perceive *lack*, and then the Universe shows us more lack because that is what we focus on. Where our attention goes, our intention follows. So, we fill our being with wanting because we want something to be different. We believe that if we want it, it will come because we want it so much. Or we believe that it will show up because we are working hard for it or because we deserve it.

Or we believe the opposite. We don't deserve it. We didn't work hard enough or only others are good enough. None of that is true. What is true is that our perception creates our reality, and to live an abundant life, we have to step into the abundant life that is already here. It exists. So why don't we just step into it?

Don't see it? Step anyway. Believe that it is here. And then step into what already exists. Think it's hard? It isn't. It's already here. How can you do this? One way is to be in gratitude for it already being here. Say, *Thank you for the wealth and abundance that is already showing up in my life. Thank you for the wealth that is already showing up tomorrow. Already* is a powerful tool that makes life easy to travel. *Already* adds conviction as well as ease to your gratitude.

The energy of wanting is not the energy of abundance. Abundance is already here, and is the energy of having. Celebrate what you already have. Then celebrate more of it. And then celebrate even more of that!

## Abundance through Joy

### Joy Scenario

The Morning Prayer practice itself leads to Abundance through Joy. I know this because it was the practice of doing the meditation on Abundance and Joy that led me to this conclusion. This isn't about the abundance of Joy or a lot of Joy. Although we shall see that the Abundance of Joy scenario works also. It is a lot like the chicken and the egg question of which came first. By that I mean that a great amount of Joy or an Abundance of Joy can create Abundance. So, I am calling this scenario *Abundance through Joy*. *Scenario* is a good word for this because we are, after all, actors on the stage of life. And the scene is Abundance through Joy.

### Wealth Follows Joy

How does the *Abundance through Joy* manifest itself? Joy begets Abundance begets Joy begets Abundance. That's a lot of begetting. And I think that is the point. Wealth can bring us happiness. But there are also a lot of wealthy people out there who aren't happy. So, Abundance it isn't about bringing us happiness. This scenario is about being happy in the first place, and then Abundance or wealth following, or not. If we are happy or Joyful in the first place, then why does it matter? The relationship has to be Joy in the first place without our Abundance necessarily following. One can't be dependent on the other. Our Joy can't be dependent on our wealth. Look at all the rich movie stars who commit suicide. One must flow from the other. Wealth must flow from Joy, and Joy must flow from Abundance for the relationship to happen.

 When we surrender to our authenticity,
our self-worth reflects abundance.

## A Flowing Relationship

Then how does this flowing relationship work? Wanting this relationship to work doesn't help matters any more than wanting a love relationship that doesn't exist. In a love relationship, you have to love yourself as you are, and only then are you ready to share yourself with another. And then the other person shows up to be in a relationship with you. You continue to flow with yourself and another or you don't.

It is the same with money and Abundance. You have to Love or be joyful about what you already have, and then the Abundance will flow toward you. Then it will show up.

## It's Good Business

It's also like a bank lending you money. They only seem to want to lend you money if you are wealthy enough not to need it. If you are desperate for a loan, they don't want to give it to you. I'm not condoning what the banks do—I guess it's just good business. What if that *just good business* works for flowing money and abundance into your life?

What if all you had to do to flow more of something, anything into your life, was to be grateful for what there already is in your life? And guess what? That's how it works. Joy is an expression of gratitude that has an element of celebration in it. Joy goes beyond a *thank you*. So, there is a little more flow when you are joyful.

Want more money or more of anything else in your life? Be a little more joyful about what you already have in that area of your life. Whether it's wealth or more fans following your blog. A couple of months ago I had one or two fans following me. Now I have 330. That may not seem like a lot to some. But I am grateful for every one of them. At night before I go to sleep, I thank the Universe for every fan who has commented on my blog and decided to follow me. The more grateful I am, the more they show up. That is how it works.

*Turn Gratitude into Joy*

We get more of what we focus on. If we focus on lack that's what we get more of. So, I focus on what I already have. And I am grateful. How do I turn grateful into Joy? I say thank you so many times that I am smiling. And I continue until I feel joyful. It is not possible to be ungrateful while you are saying *thank you*. If you need to say it a thousand times, then say it that much. Or place your hand over your heart and give heartfelt thanks. Feel it. You will be moved to Joy.

Allow money to show up however it wants to. We don't get to decide how. It can show up as a raise, as a discount, or as a coupon. It shows up in many ways. Don't discount the way it shows up by saying, *But I want you to show up by my winning the lottery*. We don't get to decide how or when. We get to stand in Joy as we watch and experience the how.

We get to be joyful as we watch it happen. Again, and again. Oh my. Again and again is the abundance of abundance. Isn't that funny!

## Abundance through Health

Abundance through Health is interesting. If we don't have our health, we sometimes say, *I have nothing*. Or we say, *What good is our wealth if we don't have our health?* But what if we have our wealth because we have our health? What I mean is that our health can actually give us wealth. So how does that work?

*Better Function*

When we are healthy, we can act and function better. We can do more things when we are healthy than if we were encumbered by being unhealthy. We can go to work more often and work longer hours. We are simply more productive. But, is being more productive bringing us more wealth? I don't think that is how we should spend our time. But we could. We could also play more and vacation more and take more time to rest. Although when we are sick, our body is making us rest. But resting because we want to rest is better than having to rest.

*Take a Break*

I took yesterday off and had a date afternoon with my husband. Red Lobster and a movie. We did it just because. It was a Wednesday and we both needed a break. So, we did. We all need to do more things like that. Have some spontaneous fun and take a break from our daily routines. How does that increase our wealth?

When our health becomes reinvigorated, our wealth also becomes reinvigorated. All aspects of our lives are reinvigorated. While I can say that it does happen. Just how and in what way it happens, I can't say. The Universe determines how and when. But I do know that it does. If you want more wealth, get more health. Take a break and have some fun. Get your rest. Eat right and exercise. Constantly working and struggling for the mighty dollar isn't going to bring you more wealth. It's just going to bring you more struggling. Work and participate. But don't turn it into a marathon.

If you are doing something that you love, you may work long hours. But then that work will invigorate you, not deplete you. Time will fly by. Your body will feel good and not tired. This kind of participation will invigorate both your body and your wealth. If what you love doing also serves others or fills a need that others have, then you will get a double return on your work investment. You will get health and abundance, because you are aligned with the intention of the universe. Abundance, Health, and service.

## Abundance through Gratitude

*Even More*

Abundance through gratitude is simple. Be grateful for what you have, and you will have even more. It's like the quote from the Bible in Matthew 13:12: "For whoever has, to him more will be given, and he will have abundance; but whoever does not have, even what he has will be taken away from him." I believe that this is about Gratitude. The more gratitude we have for what we already have, the more we are capable of receiving.

*Focus*

It isn't just about our ability to receive. It is also about our focus. When the Universe recognizes that we are grateful for what we have, then it says, *Okay. You want more of that.* When we are not grateful for what we have, and we think about what we don't have, then the Universe says, *Okay. You want more of that. You want more of what you don't have.* Place your attention and focus on what you have and be grateful for that.

## Abundance through Magic

*The Experiment*

The Universe has the ability to create whatever it wants. Whatever it intends. We experience this and we call it Magic. We align with the intention of the universe by choosing to align with Magic. I align with Magic because I like to delve into the unknown and pull a rabbit out of a hat. We are the most successful when we align ourselves with the intention of the Universe. Together we co-create the most. Magic is what we call it. But magic is not the intention of the Universe. So, what is that intention? The Universe intends to grow and evolve. To do this it experiments with what works for greater growth and evolving. It experiments with us.

*The Unknown*

Magic might seem like a poor choice for evolving. The tried, true, and proven methods might seem like better choices. But magic is an acceptance of the unknown. What we already have has gotten us to this point. But it can't grow us even further. When we align with Magic, we give the Universe permission to create for no reason. In fact, we encourage it to do so. That creation may or may not establish itself as something that endures. We won't know until we try it.

The Universe is focused on the present moment and all that is expanding. It has knowledge of the past. But it isn't controlled by it. It also doesn't look forward to the future. It only experiences the present moment through us. The universe expands and knows its Abundance through us. When you accept the unknown, you perceive more Magic. You perceive the process by which the universe is creating more of itself, more Abundance.

 We only take care of what we value.

## Abundance through Intention

*Becoming*

There is becoming and there is being. Becoming is being in a constant state of flow, whereas being is not flowing, because the energy has stopped moving. That is not bad. It is nice to take a break once in a while. To stop moving. To pull back and look around you. There is also a difference between going with the flow and allowing the flow to flow through you.

*Intention*

Intention is the focus of awareness. Awareness is looking around and seeing all the abundance that is in the Universe. Focus is saying, *How about some of that over there?* and then in the present moment saying, *Thanks. I'll have some of that and a little more of that. And thank you very much* and then stepping back into awareness and asking, *What other flavors of ice cream are there? Okay, I'll try some of that sweet basil strawberry ice cream. The chocolate I have in this moment is wonderful. But I wonder what that sweet basil strawberry tastes like?*

And then you taste a new flavor. You step into that flavor. You become the flavor you step into. Do you want more? Or *No. I think I'll go back to more kinds of chocolate. Like Chunky Munky, chocolate ice cream,* my personal favorite.

The point is that we are intentionally choosing where to put our focus. Be aware of the abundance that surrounds you. Then choose and focus on your choice. Absolute Abundance requires absolute Intention of focus.

# Abundance through Divine Perfection

*Ink Spot*

I started to write about Abundance this morning. But Ink Spot, my black cat, wouldn't let me. She kept bringing me back to present moment awareness. She kept clawing my belly from my lap. She often does that when I try to write. Or sometimes she walks across my computer. Today I asked her why she did that. I rubbed her head and came into the present moment with her. She purred. And I said, *You want me to be here now with you. I guess I can do that.* But I wanted to do something else and write. So, I put her on the floor and continued writing. Our animals often bring us into the present moment.

*Present Moment Awareness*

All things are best seen and experienced from the present moment. So, how can we be in the present moment? And what is awareness? We let go of the past. The past is in the stories we tell about it. The stories usually bring up fear or judgement. So, we let go of the stories and we let go of our fear. Fear doesn't exist in the present moment.

Then we let go of the future. We project the stories of the past into the future. So, we let go of those stories. Our anxiety melts away with the stories. What are we left with? We are left with the experience of the present moment without judgement and fear.

We become aware. What are we aware of? Everything. And from this place we can choose to experience something. How about we choose one of the higher energies like Peace or Joy? Why should we choose those energies? Because they feel better.

So why not try to hang on to the delicious feeling of Joy from the past. We don't choose to hang on to the feelings from the past because there is a sense of loss attached to them. How about the Joy of something from the future? There is always a sense of disappointment if they don't show up. It's more of a fear of disappointment. So, the only really good feeling we can have is the feeling we are having in the present moment. It is a pure energy without any sense of fear, anxiety, or disappointment attached. Be in your present moment awareness and choose.

Abundance requires us to stay in present-moment awareness, in the allowance of whatever is happening. We know that whatever is happening is in Divine Perfection. Absolute Abundance is in the celebration of Divine Perfection.

## Abundance through Purpose

Abundance simply is. It only matters what form it takes. It takes the form that we give our attention to. I give my attention to Joy and its subcategory, fun. Joy is one of the aspects of Love. When I align myself to Joy and fun, I align myself with the purpose of the Universe, to expand and evolve.

My purpose is to spread Joy to the world. I have chosen that as my purpose. The Universe's purpose for me is to enjoy the world. So, we are in alignment. My sharing my Joy is creating a greater abundance of it. So that is fulfilling my Purpose and the Universe's intent. When our intentions are in alignment, we co-create more abundance in that area. There is an abundance of joy and fun. Joy and fun work as catalysts and a place from which all other things can be created. It is much easier to create from joy than from hatred or struggle. So, more is created. More abundance of everything.

What is your purpose? Align your purpose with the purpose of the Universe.

## Abundance through Energy

What is the energy of Abundance? It is the energy of *having*. It is the energy of *It is already done*. It is the energy of *easy*. It is the energy of *There is so much in the Universe that I will never be able to sample all of the wonderful things that exist.* No matter how much I do or say or practice or experience, I can't even take out a drop of the ocean of abundance that exists. It is the energy of yes. *Yes, to all that is, and yes to me!*

We access abundance directly by accessing the energy of it. We breathe in that energy and appreciate all that is.

# Sacred Technologies of Absolute Abundance

*Techniques for Abundance through Love*

1. **Gratitude for What Is**. Say, *Thank you, Universe, for the abundance that is already in my life. Thank you. Thank you. Thank you.*
2. **Gratitude for the Future**. Say, *Thank you, Universe, for the abundance I am about to receive.*
3. **Celebrate**. Let go of wanting. Celebrate what you have. Sing and dance in that celebration.

*Techniques for Abundance through Joy*

4. **Heartfelt Gratitude.** Place your hand over your heart and feel the gratitude as you say *Thank you for …* (fill in the blank with what you already have).
5. **Relationship with Money.** Treat your money as if you were in a relationship with it. Because you are. Allow it to be whatever it wants to be and love and be joyful with it anyway. Say, *I love you anyway, money.*
6. **Whatever Way.** Then love your money however it wants to show up. Say, *Thank you for …* every time, in whatever way it shows up.

*Techniques for Abundance through Health*

7. **Day Off.** Take a day off. Do something different. Rest and Play. Whatever that means to you. Do this at least once a month.

*Techniques for Abundance through Gratitude*

8. **Past Abundance.** Make a list of all the ways you have received abundance in the past. Give gratitude for each of these things on your list.
9. **Current Abundance.** Make a list. Where do you currently see abundance around you? Give gratitude for each of these things on your list.

*Techniques for Abundance through Purpose*

10. **Listen for Purpose.** Ask what your purpose is. Say, *Universe, what is my purpose?* And then listen.
11. **Accept.** Say, *I* (state your name) *now accept that my purpose is ....*
12. **Alignment Button.** Align your purpose with the intent of the universe. Imagine that you have an alignment button on the dashboard in front of you. Hit that button and say, *I* (state your name) *now align my intention with the intention of the Universe.*

*Technique for Abundance through Energy*

13. **Energy of Abundance.** Ask the Universe to show you what Abundance feels like. Does it have a color or a taste or a smell?

# CHAPTER 6

# ABSOLUTE HEALTH

 I deserve to take care of myself.

## Absolute Health through Wellbeing

*Meditation: Tree of Life Activation*

> *I reach down into the earth with my roots. At the end of the roots, energy goes out in tiny tendrils beyond the actual root. The energy tendrils are many, and then they coalesce into a stream of energy still reaching down into the earth. The stream runs until it meets the lava that is in the center. They say hello to each other. Energy to lava. The lava is very hot. It is so hot until it seems cool. And then it seems cold. It is so cold. And then I decide that it is merely cool and maybe just the right temperature. I stay there until I feel my tree trunk rising up from the crust of the earth into the sky.*
>
> *The trunk rises up and up, and then branches out. The branches reach up. They come out to reach for the sky. Leaves form and the gentle breeze creates rustling. The leaves rustle, and the trunk and some of the branches sway. Energy reaches out from the leaves and branches, and reaches into the sky and the heavens. It goes up and up until the air and sky is infinite.*

*Then the trunk begins to swell out. It becomes as big as the universe. There is nothing else. There is just trunk.*

*I stay here for a while, and then I decide to step out. I step out and turn around to look at the tree. I look over at a drop of water. I see a tiny drop of water on a branch. As I gaze at it. I see the tree reflected in the drop of water. I touch the drop of water and put it on my lips. And then I swallow it.*

## Health and Wellbeing

Health and wellbeing. The health of our bodies is a reflection of the state of our wellbeing. It may seem like that is double talk. As though I'm saying that health is about health. But I am using *wellbeing* to include the many aspects of our lives like Joy, Peace, Love, Purpose, Gratitude Magic, Intention, and Divine Perfection. Which is to say that all the other aspects are reflected in our state of wellbeing. When we are joyful, that brings health. When we are peaceful, that brings health. All of these conditions bring health to the body, mind, and spirit. Purpose brings health to the mind and spirit. Gratitude both directly and indirectly affects our health.

When we are grateful for past health, we get more health. Where our attention goes, there goes our intention, and health follows. You might say that this level of health depends on the health of our intention. The recognition that our current state of health is in divine perfection puts us at ease. It allows us to be grateful and to go with the flow.

The health of our bodies is all about magic. Our bodies are magic in their functioning. The ability of the intention of a person's mind and spirit is certainly magical in its ability to influence the health of our body. All aspects of being and doing are at play in the wellbeing of our body, mind, and spirit. When we focus on any one aspect, such as Joy, the resulting shift is also in all other areas not just in the joy itself but also in health.

Health itself is an aspect of all the other conditions. When we focus on our health, the result is also more Joy or Peace. Of course, we are happier when we are healthy. The power of our health is to increase the power of our Joy and all other aspects or conditions. Want more Joy? Get more health. Want more health? Get more joy.

Get over yourself enough to feel good about yourself.

## Health through Love

*Mastering your Mind, Emotions, and Body*

Many healers are empaths and they can easily take on the emotions of others. This is what makes them good healers. Empaths sometimes believe that the emotions of others are their own. Like the time when I thought I was feeling the frustration of taking care of my mother when I was actually feeling her frustration of being in pain at the age of ninety-three. It was her frustration I was feeling, and not mine in taking care of her. It's easy to confuse the feelings of another with your own, especially for empaths. We need to be aware of what another is feeling. But we don't have to take it on, and we don't want to confuse their emotions with our own.

One way to know the difference is to ask ourself the question, *Is this a feeling that I choose to feel?* If *no*, then it is probably the feeling of someone else. If the answer is *yes*, then enjoy it or let it go.

*The Art of Receiving*

To exist on the earth with Health, or to just be healthy, we must be here from a different place. We are all healers. Those who call themselves healers and those who call themselves the patients. We must all perceive the conditions that surround us differently. I call that moving into another place. How do we move into this other place?

As an energy healer, we embody our soul's vibration. When working with another as a healer, we hold the space of our soul's vibration for them to experience their own soul's vibration, sometimes called the higher self. We need to embody that higher vibration. We can all do this.

We and they need to stay open to receive. Say, *I now choose to receive Love.* We create the new world in the quantum world, not in the thinking world. When we consciously breathe, we integrate the light of that world into the body.

Then we let the energy state hold us. We don't hold the energy state. It's too much work to hold the space. Instead, we let the space hold us. This is practicing the art of receiving.

Practicing the art of receiving into your heart and mind allows you to be in divine right timing. We each do our own upgrade. When we upgrade ourselves, we are loving ourselves.

 We each do our own upgrade.

# Health through Peace

*Healing through Beauty*

Every morning when I get up, I say thank you to the sunrise. It is beautiful. This morning was no exception. The extreme cold made for a cloudless sky and a very long pink sky. I live in a grey place. So, an extended sunrise is particularly appreciated. Beauty is seen both externally and internally. When we fail to see the beauty that surrounds us, we also fail to see the beauty that is inside of us.

When we see ourselves as beautiful, we are restoring ourselves to a beautiful healthy state. Health is beautiful. Beautiful is healthy. The more we look at beauty the more we become it. Seeing ourselves that way takes an act of intention or will, unless we are as a little child who is beautiful without knowing it. But that little child is beautiful because they are seeing the whole world as beautiful. They are innocent of the judgements that we learn to have as we grow up. The judgements that say that we aren't good enough. That our nose is too big, our hair is too curly, or our skin color is not the right shade.

We tend to be a society that is much more concerned about how we look based on what the media is telling us. Many of us have also bought into what the media is telling us about our health. I have probably read twenty books on why I should eat, not eat, or take this one supplement to be the healthiest person on planet earth. Now maybe that is a bit of an exaggeration. But I think you get the point. I quit taking the eighteen supplements I was on at one point, because I woke up one morning and was appalled by the number of things I was doing to be healthy.

*Harmony*

Health is also a matter of harmony or alignment with our body, which needs to be aligned with the Universe and our planet. There is a balance. That balance is a Harmony. We need to listen to our body, and then do what it tells us to do. My friend Leslie, who is a healer, says, *Your body is your guru.*

We need to learn to listen to our body about when to eat and what to eat. I'm talking about your body and not your ego-mind. What would your body like to eat? What exercise would your body like to do? I love to swim and play with my horse outside, and I love to ice skate. And I love to nap. Sometimes I love to work outside. I love to weed my garden. Do what your body loves to do. It's the balance in our lives that brings us into harmony with the earth.

*Wonder*

When we look around and see the beauty, we are also left with a state of wonder. Wonder is beyond asking a question like *I wonder what would happen if ….* It is standing in the exquisite beauty of the Universe and being in awe.

*The Wonder of a Tree from Beyond Joy*

How does a tree feel peace? A tree just is. Presence comes to mind. A tree is present and then it isn't. What is the wisdom of a tree? It hears all things and speaks to those who are willing to listen. What does it say?

> *I am rooted in the earth and spread my branches into the heavens, and I share in the glory of God as sun shines down on me and the wind blows and trims my branches. I drink from the earth, and rain washes away the dust. I hear the music of the earth and of all living things. I even hear the music of you humans who can be so lost. You don't need to be lost. You can awaken to my presence. Awaken to your own presence.*

We breathe out and the tree breathes in our carbon dioxide. It breathes out oxygen, which we breathe in. We breathe the best in each other's presence. It's almost as if we breathe in a tree's exhale and it breathes in our exhale. We are breathing each other.

The tree is sharing its breath and its wonder with us. This high vibrational state raises our vibrational state. We are in harmony with our surroundings. We stand in harmony, beauty, and yes, Health.

 Feeling good allows you to access and
handle the pressure of having gifts.

# Health through Joy

### Health and Breath

When we laugh and are joyful, we naturally have all those chemicals in our bodies that make us healthy. Laughter—which is an expression of Joy—provides the health benefits of improved blood flow, lower levels of the stress hormone cortisol, and a more efficient immune system. Joy brings us Health.

The link between Health and our breath is also easy for me to see. We can't live without the breath. Breathing is inspiration, the breathing in of the spirit. So, breath is necessary for the body and the mind.

### The Breath Influences Our Lives.

Breathing moves energy. Watching your breath as it moves is one way to control the movement of energy. When you align your breath with energy, you can direct the energy to follow the movement of your breath. You give it a direction, and then you are controlling the flow of your energy. When you control the flow of energy in your life, you control the substance in your life because energy precedes substance. Influence your breath. Influence your energy and influence your life

There are lots of yogic breathing techniques out there, many of which I have practiced over the years. I've also offered "The seven seconds of breathing" as a practice in a few of my blogs and my books. "The seven seconds of breathing" exercise is good for anxiety and good for centering. And it has many health benefits.

> *Western mystics, Indian yogis, Taoist sages have known for millennia that breathing is a pathway to higher levels of consciousness. Most people don't realize that not breathing optimally limits our physical energy and quality of life but also our ability to access those deepest spiritual levels of our being.*

> —THE TRANSFORMATIONAL BREATH FOUNDATION

Science has shown us that there are psychological functions like cognition, performance, wellbeing, and physical disorders that can be enhanced or improved through various breathwork practices. So why not breathe consciously? You have to breathe anyway. Conscious breathing takes you a step further.

> *The Breath facilitates movement.*

> —ZACH REHDER

### Conscious Breathing

Conscious breathing is breathing in the flow of awareness. It is an emotional detox. It is also called transformational breathwork, shamanic breathwork, and holotropic breathwork.

Transformational breathwork, according to the Transformational Breath Foundation, can increase wellbeing, raise cognition, and reduce performance anxiety. Transformational breath is clearly experienced on the physical, mental, and emotional levels. It also operates on the level of causality—spirit, where real healing takes place—which ultimately makes it a Spiritual modality.

Conscious breathing is a technique I have practiced for a few years. It involves a circular breath. That means no stopping at the top and bottom of the breath. One pulls the breath in and lets it drop out very quickly. You don't push it out. That would lead to hyperventilation. This practice can be done with a group and an instructor or alone for a few minutes. You could do ten breaths this way, and then journal about it. Particularly if you set yourself up with a question before you get started. Like, *What is going on with my body here? My knee, my stomach, foot, or eye?* Ask the question. Do the breathing, and then listen for the answer.

Asking the question in and of itself is also a good practice. *What is going on in this part of my body?* Name that part and then listen. You can journal about it or not depending on where you are or what you are doing. If you like to journal, then journal. If you like to meditate, then do that. Tying the breath to this practice only deepens it.

Find a conscious breathing expert near you. There are now many breathing experts who practice online. You can try one of them.

### Breath Practitioners

- Zach Rehder: www.zachrehder.com
- Rosanna Lo Meo Peachy: www.NewBeginningsWithRosanna.com
- Fiorella Garibaldi: www.fiorellagaribaldi.com

 Let your health go viral.

### Magnificence and Health

Magnificence and its influence on our Health is a little harder to envision. *Envision* is the right word because we can envision our health, and we envision the magnificence of something. I've defined *Magnificence* as extreme simplicity or extreme repetitive complexity or the in-between beauty of a sunset that has gone viral in the sky. Gone viral. That's a description of Magnificence, beauty gone viral. It is beauty so wonderful that it has gone viral to itself. It is so pure in what it is that its own perfect self explodes out to the world.

This is where we can see the relationship to our health. Magnificence is the expression of the purity of the person or object. And that purity is expressed outward to the world. The purity of our health expressed outward to the world. We are what we choose to see. When we see the magnificence of a sunset, we become that magnificence. And the purity of it affects the purity of what we are. We are as pure as that sunset. The opposite is also true. When we look at the muck of the crap that is also present in the world, we reflect that muck also.

We have a choice about what we choose to look at. We need to be aware of the junk that is out there, but we can also choose to look at and stand in the Magnificence of the world. What we are is what we choose to see. This would hold true of Magnificence also.

The purity of magnificence has gone viral with itself. And then it goes viral with the world. We need to let the purity of ourselves go viral within us.

### Breathe in the Magnificence

So, what happens when you breathe in the magnificence of the universe or a sunrise? You breathe in the magnificence that you see. You begin to embody it. That embodiment is allowing yourself to be in a state of Absolute Health. That is a state where, unlike cancer, all of your cells are going viral in their own purity. Why not breathe that in! Isn't that Magnificence Joyful!

## Health through Gratitude

### Gratitude for Past Health

This morning I was meditating on "Gratitude for Health." I thanked myself for the times in my past when I was especially healthy. I remembered when I had a "forty and gorgeous" birthday party. I had lost weight and I wore a very Spanish-looking, off-the-shoulder ruffled dress. We were living overseas in Western Samoa. My husband was the director of the Peace Corps there, and we had something akin to embassy status. I had invited some of the ambassadors and high-ranking expatriate officials to my party. I truly felt gorgeous and healthy. Of course, I worked out every day. I played tennis, golf, and pumped iron. I had a fish diet and ate very little junk food. So, I told myself that there was good reason for my health. I thanked myself and the Universe for being healthy. *Thank you, thank you, thank you.*

I thought about "fifty and nifty" and "sixty and sexy." I thought that "sixty and sexy" was the next time when I really felt healthy. I had named each of my birthday milestones so that I would feel better when they came. But in truth, I didn't really notice them. They simply came and went.

My next healthy time that I noticed was when a fellow teacher at the college where I taught said, *One of your students told me that you never miss a day at work. In fact, you haven't missed a day for the last ten years.* That was true. I hadn't had a cold or flu or missed any work. But I did tend to take my health for granted. I thought that I just had healthy genes. Which I do. And now I thank the universe for that good health. *Thank you. Thank you. Thank you.*

Around "sixty and sexy," I lost thirty pounds by going on a diet. I did feel healthy and beautiful. At that time, I swam forty minutes of laps every day before work. Again, I thank the Universe for my good health. *Thank you. Thank you. Thank you.*

I started this morning with my Morning Prayer. I knew that I was going to choose Gratitude this morning because I had decided to do gratitude every day for ninety days to see what happens.

*I choose gratitude for my current state of health. Thank you, thank you, thank you.*

*Health Meditation*

> *I check out my body. There is something going on behind my heart chakra. I open up the area. I open a big hole, like a donut. Water comes gushing through and out the front. It is like a river of water coming through. Dolphins and whales fly and swim through the opening. And then all sorts of animals are hanging around on the edges. Even Gollum is climbing around the edges as if it were a huge cave. I think, "Why should only the good animals be a part of my world?" After* all love contains all things. And all things are a part of us.

*I check out the spot behind my heart and it is no longer there.*
*I wonder what will happen if I increase the size. Instead of*
*just around my heart, I open it to all the way down to my root*
*chakra. Everything is vibrating wildly. Then I see a doorway.*
*It is no longer a round opening, but a doorway. It is full of*
*blinding light. I walk through it.*

What was the door that I stepped through? It was the door of gratitude. *Thank you. Thank you. Thank you.* To encourage good health, we must not take the health we currently have for granted. Thank the universe for your past good health. Thank it for whatever part of you is currently healthy. And then thank the universe for the perfect health that you already have in the future.

## Health through Magic

*Sacred garden*

This morning's vision started like so many recently where I am on a stage.

*I am on a stage, and the stage is my sacred garden. I am*
*explaining to the group that is the audience about our happy*
*places, and the place we could call our sacred garden. For*
*me, it seems to be the stage. I find that I journey from there.*
*I explain about the lower world and communing with the*
*animal spirits there. I explain about the upper world and*
*communing with guides and angels that reside there. I*
*explain about what I call the middle earth. I pay homage to*
The Lord of the Rings. *The middle world is about the world*
*we live in, and in that place also exist the multiverses. One*
*song is a universe, and many songs comprise the multiverse.*
*This is the place where we step into other dimensions.*

*I stand back and part the veil with my hands in a slicing*
*motion. I step into the world where dragons live. Then I step*
*back and turn slightly to the right. I slice again and I step*

*into the world of fairies. But, No, I say, and step back again. I choose the world of dragons. So, I step into that world.*

*Then I decide to play with the elements. I look at earth. It is made of matter and minerals and gemstones and also the dark soil in which we grow our food. It also contains wood and plants. Then I look at water. It is fluid and moving. I hear the wind and it moves and creates the movement. I think of air and my breath. I see fire. It creates energy and is formed by light. It is energizing.*

## Dragon Clothes

*I decide to create a person from these elements. I whip up all four elements into a maelstrom. And I see what I have created, but it is just a mud baby. So, I let it go. It dissipates.*

*Then I decide to create a dragon. I whip up the earth first because it is made of matter. And then I add water. The dragon becomes fluid. Then I add air and the dragon has motion. Then I add fire and the dragon has energy and breath. I decide to play with the beauty of it and add gemstones for the eyes and mica for the scales and a beautiful gilded saddle.*

*Then I stand back to see what I have created. I ask the spirit of Dragon to enter what I have made. She does. She stretches into the form and I ask her how she likes it. She makes the legs longer and does some other adjusting. Spirit has no form. And now she has one.*

*I climb on board. I ask the group to join me in flying off. Or, I say that they can just sit with their dragon or the animal that they have created.*

*I suggest that they fly to their home planet or anywhere they choose. I am going to the heart of God, because I can. I tell them they are welcome to join me there.*

*I sit in the heart of God. My spirit dragon stands off to the right. It is quiet. There is nothing.*

> *I wait and then I decide it is time to go. I climb back on my dragon and I tell the others that they can return home when they are ready. Upon returning, I give my dragon a rose and say, "Thank you." I ask her for a final message. She says, "Be at Peace on your path my child." Then she sheds the garment that I made. I hang it up in a closet to reuse at a later date. All forms are just clothes that we wear.*
>
> *I know that my own form is just clothing made from the elements of earth, water, fire, and wind. I feel my own minerals and matter, the water that makes up 90 percent of my body and the air that gives movement. The fire burns as my synapses fire, and I am energized. I am made up of the elements and I am energized. But these are just the clothes that my spirit wears. In the end I will hang them up in God's closet.*

We can put on our health in the same way that we wear our clothes. We might call this magical. And it is.

## Health through Intention

Last night I said to John, *Just once I would like to go out on New Year's Eve and wear a sparkly dress instead of a flannel shirt and jeans.* I had just seen a sequined dress on the television that I liked. I was reminded of a meditation that I had, sitting and wearing a flannel shirt.

*Meditation: An OBE Trip*

> *I run energy through me. As I am waking up, I see a being in a flannel shirt. I decide that the being is me. I am onstage in Sedona. I sit in a chair. I demonstrate an OBE double.* [This is an out-of-body experience energy body. It is also sometimes called a double or bilocation double.] *I watch it as it shapeshifts. It shifts into a unicorn then a dragon and then a phoenix. How easy it is. Then I create a thousand*

*doubles of myself. They are all around the auditorium. Then they stand in front of each individual in the audience. There is one double for each person sitting in the auditorium. I take the hand of each person sitting, and I take the whole group to Paris. We walk down the Champs-Élysées. We eat cream puffs. Then we go to the base of the pyramid of Cheops in Egypt. Then we come back to the auditorium. And I say, "See how easy it is?"*

I guess I don't need a sparkly dress to go to Paris and eat cream puffs. My flannel shirt will get me there just fine. But why do I think that I need a sparkly dress? To be beautiful? But I already am beautiful in my flannel shirt. I guess I was reacting to listening to the message on the television, that said I needed one to be beautiful. I think I can let that message go. And maybe I will wear one anyway. I remember a dean at the college where I taught saying, *You can't have too many sparkly dresses or be too thin.* I'm not either. And that's okay. I will ring in the new year in whatever costume strikes me as fitting in the moment.

## Beauty and Healing

Healing can contain any or all of the thirty aspects and conditions that I have described in the thirty-some chapters in my books. They range from Breath to Wonder. This morning in my meditation I wondered about beauty and its relationship to healing. This is only one aspect of many. But the intention that we have concerning beauty directs the intention we have about our health. Therefore, I think that it is relevant to this chapter on Intention and Health.

 There's no one here preventing me from feeling good about myself.

When we see someone whom we call beautiful, what we are really seeing is the beauty that they are on the inside. This is their inner beauty shining out.

And sometimes when we see someone who should look beautiful because they are an actress or model and everything seems to be just the right ... whatever ... to be called beautiful, but somehow, we don't see them as beautiful, we wonder, *Why is that?* What is missing that we don't see them as beautiful?

Is beauty missing from them or us? Yes, to both.

But this description is about the *missing from them* part first. I think that they don't look beautiful because they are not radiating the beauty that is inside them. They are radiating hate, envy, or fear. A beautiful person radiates Love and Joy or Peace. They also radiate Health. We see them as beautiful and healthy.

## Color of Health

We think of healthy as beautiful. Healthy and beautiful are not the same condition, but they are related. Beauty can be the color lavender. Peace can be the blue component. Lavender is made up of pink and blue. Pink is Joy and blue is Peace. What if Health were white and not lavender?

Or maybe Health is gold. Shining out. And there are lavender components and orange and Green and many colors that make up our health. What we radiate out is what others see or are capable of seeing. Sometimes they can only see through dark-colored glasses that only let in certain shades of a color. Some people can only see hate and greed. Some, a very few, can only see love. Like the Dalai Lama. We all wear glasses. I prefer his rose-colored glasses.

What happens if we shine so brightly that even their dark-colored glasses can't keep the light out? They may see the light that we are bringing to the world. And they may find the way home to themselves. We call this healing and being healed in an energetic sense. But it is more than energy because it affects the physical, mental, and spiritual worlds. It affects our mind, body, and spirit. We say that *when we heal others, we heal ourselves. When we heal ourselves, we heal others*. And that is true because when another finds his way home to himself, then the whole world has upshifted just a little bit, and then we too are upshifted a little bit. And we shine even brighter. So, healing has taken place.

Another person is attracted to that energy because its higher self recognizes the high energy and is attracted to it even if the person doesn't know why he is attracted to you. He is attracted in spite of his ego-mind self. He is attracted to letting go of his separation energy.

Beauty is just one color, one hue, of Health. And health is a component of beauty. They have the same relationship that yin and yang have to each other. Not in an opposite sense but in a physical relationship sense with one inside the other. Beauty like yin is at the heart of yang and Health like yang is at the heart of yin. Not opposite of, but in the heart of. Beauty and health are each in the heart of the other.

## Health through Divine Perfection

*Caring*

I was thinking this morning about what *caring* means. And why I continually question that I am a Life Coach. I call myself and am certified as a Life Transformed Coach. But what is coaching anyway? I question my ability to be a coach because I don't seem to have the character traits of many coaches. I don't seem to be compassionate, and what many would call caring. I don't commiserate. In fact, I don't do misery in any form, let alone *com-miserate*. Empaths can be aware of someone else's misery without stepping into it and joining them. So how can I be a coach? I also don't do one-on-one coaching sitting down in a room, which I consider to be the usual format.

What do I do? I write books, I speak on stage, and I do classes online and in person. In those instances, I seem to be coaching one on one. So, there is some of that. I do Zoom conferences. So, okay, I guess I do one-on-one coaching also. *Argh!* Why do I struggle so with this?

I feel like an egg-sucking dog who comes running up to you with egg yolk running down his chin and says, *What egg? I don't see any eggs.*

*The Perfect Path*

I struggle because I don't like to tell people what to do. Or how they should be. I don't want to take away their perfect path that is already teaching them what they need to know to move on, if they would only see it that way. And therein lies the problem. They don't see it that way.

They believe that they are wrong or need fixing and changing. They believe that they need help to make those changes. And here I am to help them see that they don't need anybody's help to make the changes. And that they are already making those changes by asking for the help. They have already started the process.

To call myself a coach seems disingenuous in the process. But there you have it. I am called many things, *Dream Maker of Worlds, Joy Magnet. Joy Wizard. Energy Alchemist, Energy Weaver,* and *Energy Dancer.* Oh, and I am also called a *Life Transformed Coach.* I can see another's struggles because I can see that I also struggle. I am not perfect. I am not without some struggle. I struggle with calling myself a coach and believing that I am good enough or have anything to offer.

## Allowance

So, what do I think about caring? True caring is total allowance. Allowing people to go through what they have chosen to learn on their path. I am here to help them get back up when they appear to have stumbled. I help them to align their energy with their chosen path. Allowance sometimes does not look like compassion. But it is. When we allow, we give the other person the benefit of knowing they have the ability to change.

When we pity or feel sorry for them, we take away their dignity and disempower them. Allowance is empowering. Caring is empowering. I can do that. And for me, coaching is about allowance and empowering without judgement. Judgement disempowers. I guess I can let go of my own not-good-enough-to-be-a-coach persona who cares through allowance without judgement.

Healing through Divine Perfection is recognizing that we are already on the perfect paths to experience disease and heal ourselves. Sometimes as healers we get to watch it happening in others. We are observers. Sometimes we get to observe it in ourselves. We are all healers no matter what we do. We are all life coaches no matter what we do.

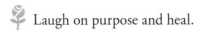 Laugh on purpose and heal.

# Health through Purpose

## *Laughter and Healing*

I've written a lot about how laughter heals. Many people have. How laughter releases endorphins and lowers our blood pressure. There is no doubt that a good belly laugh is good for us. But now I want to ask the opposite question. Can healing make us laugh? Is any of it funny?

I find much of it absurd. Is absurd funny? Odd maybe. The definition for *absurd* is "wildly unreasonable, illogical, or inappropriate." The synonyms are "preposterous, ridiculous, ludicrous, farcical, laughable, idiotic, stupid, foolish, and silly." So, when we do something absurd, it is laughable. What is it that's absurd about healing?

## *Absurd or Reasonable*

There was a time in my life when I rejected Western medicine. I still did my obligatory yearly checkup. But I didn't do much else. But I was also taking a lot of extra vitamins and supplements. One multivitamin had six pills in it alone. One day I looked in the mirror as I was taking the supplements and said to myself, *This is absurd.* But I wasn't laughing. I stopped right then and there. No more supplements. My doctor tells me that I should take a multivitamin pill. He wanted me to take one and I was taking eighteen. I guess I'm just an overachiever.

I would read a book about health and then I would supplement. One week it was coconut oil. The next week it was vitamin E. Then D and then A. Or it was cumin or turmeric or Goji berries. Maybe it's kombucha or some enzyme. I'm not saying that any of these things are bad. Nor am I saying that any of these things are good. We read a book and we believe. The power of the arguments convinces us. And they do work.

Or perhaps we give something up like gluten or grains. We believe that they do something or don't do something and then that works. It all seems to work. It all does work.

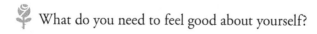 What do you need to feel good about yourself?

## Simplicity

It's just that my life was getting too complicated. And I like simple. No complications. So, I gave it all up. I just listen to my body and it says, *How about this?* I am having ice cream and chocolate or I am having a salad or a steak or I am having nothing whatsoever.

I am not saying that you shouldn't see your doctor. See your doctor and do what she or he tells you to do. Or not. It's your choice. Make it an informed and conscious choice. What I am saying is that we have a choice about what we do and that we should listen to our bodies and do what they tell us to do.

## Beliefs

Doctors of both Western medicine and the gurus of alternative medicine believe in what they are practicing. There is truth in both. The truth lies in the power of the energy of the belief. When I read a book, by the end of it I believe what they are saying, if it is reasonable. (There are some books out there that are totally whacko. But I wouldn't read more than a chapter or two in one of those.) I do what the book says. I practice it for a while. It works and then I get bored and move on. Or maybe I just don't need to do it anymore. Maybe it has done what it needed to do, and I moved on.

It isn't right or wrong to try something for a while. It is just an experience. Isn't it funny that we live life having these experiences? And it is our purpose to experience life. Experience life well or experience life sick. Or somewhere in between. It is just a continuum of experiences in wellness or sickness. We do have a choice.

In Ojai, California, a few weeks ago, I told my friend Barbara that I wasn't having a cold. She was concerned about coming down with a cold that her husband just had. She was taking this or that supplement. She thought about what I just said that I wasn't having a cold. And she thought, *Hmm, you aren't choosing it.* Well, she wasn't either. But she was choosing not having it from a place of fear of having it. Fear of having something is not the same as choosing to not have it. Fear can bring it toward us because we are concentrating on what it is that we don't want to have.

Remember the Universe doesn't hear *no*. It doesn't hear *I don't want;* it only hears *I want.*

Be careful what you don't want and focus on what you do want. I want health. I want perfect health. What if it were that easy? What if all we have to do were to choose perfect health? Now that's funny. Our purpose is to experience life. I choose to experience a healthy life.

 The bees dance to tell their story. They tell how far and in what direction the pollen is. Also, how good the pollen is.

## Health through Energy

*How Lightworkers Heal*

As healers, we create a space where the individual can do his own healing. All we have to do is be in a space of receiving and allow Source to flow through us. Then we sometimes take the mind of the other person along. How we take the mind along varies from one lightworker to the next. We take them through our belief system and away from their own. For the most part, we assist them in letting go of their limiting beliefs. But we also install and instill our own beliefs. It can be difficult to let go of all beliefs. It sometimes seems easier to let go of limiting beliefs by expanding our awareness.

Darius Barazandeh, founder of The You Wealth Revolution, says that we lead others up to the place where they can jump in the pool and swim in it. We don't tell them *This is how you do it*, although we can offer some exercises that worked for us.

Many times, in a transformational class we hear statements like, *My cat got run over and I'm trying to deal with that.* So, often the coach will try to fix the emotion that has implanted itself because of the event. But the person needs to find their own pool to swim in to receive the energy. Then they need to know that they can simply receive that energy and then they can embody it in every cell, organ, and tissue of their body. They then can bring the source energy into form. And that will "inform" their way of acting in the world.

Lightworkers have a variety of ways of activating the energy field of what Kenji Kumara, energy healer of Quantum Lightweaving, calls the Quantum. I call it Source or God. As lightworkers, we open up another person to the Source for all and the source of themselves so that they can be their own energy master. We are really offering them the energy to inform their souls. Or to embody their souls. Or to align their souls with their physical being. All of these are ways of perceiving what happens.

When we try to hold the space of Love, it becomes a lot of work and sometimes we empathically take on another's malady. But if we allow Source to hold us in the space of Love, then there is no effort. As lightworkers, we are fully supported and so is the individual we are assisting.

*Receiving Energy*

Holding the space of Love is the state of receiving. The energy of receiving must be allowed to flow freely through us. Then we expand it to another or a whole room of others. We cannot hold onto it. It must be allowed to flow. We can direct it. We intend it to go to our hearts or wherever we believe it needs to go to heal or align with our desires. We can do this when we are working on ourselves.

From the place of Source, we can flow the energy to our finances, our relationships, or our body. We can flow it anywhere. We can also step back and watch where it goes without any direction.

In working with another, it is advisable to step back and watch. We do not know better than God or the individual himself where the energy needs to go. What we add to the present moment situation is the *energy of receiving*. The more we are open to our own receiving, the more openness we have to share with another person's energy of receiving. Then their own higher power heals them in the most efficient way.

We might think that they need more peace in their life. But when we watch, we see that more struggle is flowing in. Perhaps the individual needs more lessons of struggle to progress. We don't know. Only their own soul knows what they need. We are allowed to watch and add the energy of receiving to speed the process along.

## Removing the Blocks to Energy

First, energy has to move. It can't be contained. We have to allow it to move. We do that by unblocking it. We also have to close down the leaks in our body's energy field. Then we can store it and increase it. Then we can dance with it. Then we can weave it and manifest with it.

## First Steps First

First, we need to get energy moving and unblock it. And plug the holes. Unblocking and plugging the holes seem to be at odds with each other as concepts. But they aren't. There can be many blocks. But the big ones are pain, emotions, and beliefs.

Pain can be a block to moving energy. It is both a block and a fiery energy leak at the same time. It blocks us from where we want to go by removing our focus from one direction and pulling us to it. But pain just wants to be released. Take your focus to that part of your body. Enter it and relax into it and let it go. Take a deep breath as you do this. Breathe into it and out through it. This will release some if not all of the fiery energy that is leaking out of that spot.

I have already also written about a myriad of exercises like *the accordion* and *the lasso*. Try any of these to ease your pain.

Change your beliefs from negative ones to positive ones, and get your energy moving a little. When you change your belief from, *I can't do this* to *I can do this*, you are getting the energy moving.

If you let go of all beliefs and operate from that place, you really get the energy moving. That would be like *I have no beliefs about what I can or can't do. And I choose to do this anyway.* Now the energy really gets moving. There are no positive or negative limitations on what you can do. Both conditions put your energy in a box and contain it.

After beliefs come the blocks of emotions. Emotions are energy in motion. So, the energy is moving, but is it moving in the direction that you want it to go? We can change the energy of our emotions by changing or letting go of the stories that fuel them. Story is what creates, sustains, and fires up our emotions. That is why a good movie or book can uplift our spirits. And why gossip and the story that we tell ourselves about something can leave us in the dirt. Feeling low, or angry.

 Story unites us. It is a bus that travels
around and makes a connection.

### Story

We create our own story. Why not make it a good one? What if you could write the story that you want to live? You can! Let go of all existing story and write a new one.

This is the beginning of playing with energy. Remove your blocks and get your energy flowing by changing or letting go of your beliefs, changing your emotions, and allowing your energy to flow. When you master your energy, you master your health and your life.

## Sacred Technologies of Absolute Health

### Techniques for Health through Love

1. **Increase Receiving**. Say three times, *I now choose to receive …* (insert *Love, health* or *wealth*). Say whatever you would like to receive. You could also say, *I choose to receive receiving.*
2. **Receiving Breath.** Breathe in slowly and out slowly as you count to seven seconds. Do this seven times. Feel the energy of receiving as you inhale and feel yourself letting go as you exhale.

### Techniques for Health through Peace

3. **Food Awareness.** Eat your food with the intention of nourishing your body. Eat with the intent of pleasure. Ask God what the food tastes like. Listen with your awareness.
4. **Wonder.** Ask yourself how a plant or a tree feels. Do they have peace or Joy or beauty or abundance or power? What is it that the plant reflects in you?

5. **Expand Your Energy** in and out. Shrink your energy field in as small as you can make it into your center. Then expand it out as big as the Universe. Coordinate its expansion and contraction with your inbreaths and outbreaths. Don't just contract in to your normal size of energy field. Contract your energy into a center that goes in as far as the Universe goes out. Now that's really falling into yourself!

6. **Cocoon.** Once you have your energy moving with the in-and-out exercise above, unzip the front of your energy cocoon and step out.

7. **Let Go of Another's Energy.** Say, *Everything that doesn't belong to me, now leave.* And then fill the space with gratitude. Say, *I wonder how much gratitude I can feel.*

8. **Wonder.** Ask yourself, *How much can I Wonder? What does Wonder feel like?*

9. **Mirror Work.** Look in a mirror. Tell yourself that you are beautiful. Find something that you can believe. If you like your hair, tell yourself that you have beautiful hair. Do this for a few minutes. Do this every day. Then change to something else that you find beautiful. As you do this more often, what you see as beautiful will change. Do this every day. Maybe as you brush your teeth.

10. **A Place of Beauty.** Sit in a place of exquisite beauty or listen to music of exquisite beauty. Ask it why it is so beautiful. And listen to the answer. Know that it is only the reflection of your own exquisite beauty. Then ask yourself how you feel.

11. **Structured Water Flow.** Flow energy down your spine as if you were a huge tube, as if you were a structured water filter. Send the energy across each chakra, where you have placed a ball. Swirl the energy around those balls clockwise and counterclockwise. Start the energy at your heart chakra and send the energy out and around in all directions. Work your way up and down your chakras. This exercise will get your energy flowing. Do at least three times.

12. **Triangle Energy.** Move your energy in a triangle. Open your palms and see the sun above your head, and your mind and spirit in your palms. Circulate the energy around the triangle. The apex

is the sun energy. Your right hand is your mind energy. Your left hand is your spirit or heart energy. Move the energy around the triangle in one direction and then in the other. Do at least three times. This will get your energy moving. It will also put your heart in your mind and your mind in your heart or spirit.

13. **Connect Health to Breath**. Breathe in and out slowly as you count to seven seconds. Do this seven times. Feel the energy of perfect health as you inhale and feel yourself letting go of dis-ease as you exhale.

14. **Yogic Breathing**: Try breathing in through your nose for a count of eight, hold for six seconds and breathe out through your nose for a count of six. Hold out for a count of four. Repeat ten times.

15. **Conscious Breathing** (the circular breath) Pull the breath in through your mouth and let it drop out very quickly. Don't push it out. There is no pause at the top or bottom of the breath. Do this for fifteen breaths or for ten minutes. Ask a question about your health. Listen for the answer. Journal or meditate about it.

16. **Breathing Expert**. Find a conscious breathing expert near you. There are now many breathing experts who practice online. You can try one of those.

17. **Breathe the Magnificence**. Look at something you believe is magnificent. Like a sunrise, sunset, the ocean, or a tree. Breathe in its magnificence. Sit with it for 10 minutes. Journal or meditate on it.

18. **Focus on Magnificence.** Look to see the magnificence in the world. Be aware of but let go of anything you think is junk. Put the junk in your peripheral vision and put your focus on magnificence.

19. **Concertina Accordion Breath.** Breathe in and out like a concertina accordion going in and out. Pretend that you are holding a small six-inch-by-six-inch concertina accordion in your hands. Breathe in and out with it as you pull and push the concertina in and out. Do this until your breath is in harmony with the action of the concertina. Then place the concertina over some part of your body that has a pain. Like your knee. Breathe in and out as you play your imaginary concertina over and through your knee. Let the concertina breathe your knee. Let your knee

breathe the concertina. Try it with any part of your body that hurts. Do this for five minutes. (See further instructions for this practice at heartachetojoy.com/accordion-breath.)

20. **Breathing the Chakras.** Take a deep breath and feel who you are, and then take a deep breath into each chakra starting at the root and working your way up to the crown chakra to discover what each chakra's energy is. Then breathe yourself and breathe that chakra until you and it are not separate. You are the same. Do this with each chakra and then move on to the next one.

21. **Breathe a Gemstone.** Use the same technique as you used in breathing the chakras. Breathe yourself and breathe the gemstone until you merge.

22. **Feel, Breathe, and Release.** Try seeing a negative feeling such as anger or sadness through the lens of divinity and awareness. First, you feel it. Then you take a deep breath and let it go.

23. **Breathe the Breath of God.** Breathe yourself and then breathe God. Do this until there is only one of you.

24. **Expanding in**. Practice expanding yourself into the core of your being on your inbreath and expand out to normal size on your outbreath. Then reverse the inbreaths and outbreaths with the practice.

25. **Internal Source Point.** Practice breathing your internal source point. Breathe while you focus your attention on your center.

*Techniques for Health through Gratitude*

26. **Past Health**. Say three times, *Thank you, Universe, for my past good health. Thank you, thank you, thank you.*

27. **Find Something Healthy.** Say three times, *Thank you, Universe, for my healthy ...* (fill in the blank).

28. **Allow.** Say three times, *Thank you, Universe, for the perfect health that I already have.*

*Techniques for Health through Intention*

29. **See Beauty** in all things. Tell everything that you see that it is beautiful. Look around you and for ten minutes tell everything that it is beautiful.

30. **Most Beautiful.** List the ten most beautiful things that you saw today.

31. **Tell Another**. Tell another person how beautiful they are. In person or in writing.

32. **Allow Beauty.** Allow your own beauty to shine forth. Your beauty will heal all those around you. Say, *By the law of divine grace and all that is light, I now allow my own beauty to shine forth.*

33. **Accept Beauty**. Say, *By the law of divine grace and all that is light, I* (state your name) *now accept the beauty that I am.*

34. **A Reflection.** Say, *By the law of divine grace and all that is light, I* (state your name) *accept that the beauty that others see in me is only the reflection of their own beauty.*

*Techniques for Health through Purpose*

35. **Choice.** Say three times, *By the law of divine grace and all that is light, I* (state your name) *now choose perfect health.*

36. **Listen.** Say three times, *By the law of divine grace and all that is light, I* (state your name) *listen to my body.*

37. **Conscious Choice.** Say three times, *By the law of divine grace and all that is light, I* (state your name) *make conscious and informed choices about my health.*

# CHAPTER 7

# ABSOLUTE GRATITUDE

 Gratitude is the catalyst that creates magic.

## Gratitude of Gratitude

*Journey: The Daisy*

I ask about the plant world. *What about the flowers? Where do they live?* Of course, they live in our world of Middle Earth. But is there also a daisy in the lower world? One who energetically represents all other flowers? Yes. But she also exists in this world.

> *Daisy looks down at all her sisters. One is farther apart from the sea of flowers. She is missing a petal. Does she feel less than the whole of her sisters because she is missing a petal? Does Daisy love her any less? Does she not belong? Does she believe that she doesn't belong?*
>
> *Is the way in which a daisy procreates and spreads her seeds bad because it is different from the dandelion? Are her seeds any less successful? What if an animal eats the seed? Are they not then left in a bed of nurturing material? Is any of it less than or greater than in her world? Does she have any beliefs about what is greater than or less than? No. It is all Glorious.*

The plant world lives in the Glory and Wisdom of the Universe. Plants listen and they celebrate with their own singing. If you haven't listened to the plants sing in our earthly world, you can listen to *Spreading Like Wildflowers, A Sonic Bouquet from Colorado*, produced by Peter May from The Sonic Apothecary, Nature Fusion Music.

When we resist anything, we are really resisting Glory. What do I mean by that? When we let go of resistance to something (like *I am not pretty enough*), we are really resisting what seems to be on the other side, Glory. It isn't on any other side. It really is already here. But we don't know that. So how do we access that glory?

First, we acknowledge what we feel or believe. We say, *Okay, I am not pretty. So, what!* Then comes *I accept that I am not pretty.* Then comes *I feel really good even though I am not pretty.* Then comes *I am joyful even if I am not … what?* At this point we begin to lose what we were resisting. Then comes *I am celebrating how I look; I am …. I am gloriously … what? I am beautiful.* Oops. How did that happen? How could I ever have thought that I wasn't pretty enough. I was simply resisting being gloriously … whatever. (You fill in the blank.)

I selected the Morning Prayer cards of *Gratitude, Caring,* and *Glory* this morning, and wondered what I could write about them that I hadn't already written. Then I recognized that these are the perfect triumvirate. It seems that I have said *accept, allow, give gratitude,* and then *celebrate* so many times. These are the stages of Gratitude.

*Acceptance*

When something negative occurs, the first step is acceptance. Acceptance is acknowledging that something is occurring. Wikipedia says that "Acceptance in human psychology is a person's assent to the reality of a situation, recognizing a process or condition (often a negative or uncomfortable situation) without attempting to change it or protest it. The concept is close in meaning to acquiescence, derived from the Latin *acquiēscere* (to find rest in)." I like that phrase "to find rest in," because when we accept something, we can then actually let go of the anxiety we were holding onto by not accepting what has happened.

*Allowance*

Allowance is the next step. By allowance I mean letting go of resistance. Resistance is when we keep trying to ignore, stop, or change what is occurring. To allow is to permit or authorize. We are reluctant participants. But we are participants. Allowance has a little more movement forward than acceptance.

*Gratitude*

After we have allowed and participated in some event, we are ready to give thanks for what has occurred. We are ready to be grateful. We can finally see that there is a silver lining, that if the event hadn't occurred, like the death of a spouse, we never would have …. Fill in the blank. We would not have taken care of the responsibilities that our spouse did. We would not have learned of our power to do some things we had never done before. We now have the freedom to travel and pursue the things we had always wanted to try but never had the time or freedom to do. We learn many life lessons with a loss or a negative occurrence. It is those lessons that we are grateful for. We are not grateful for the loss itself. Or for whatever the negative occurrence is. We are grateful for the life lessons and the opportunities that the lesson brings.

*Be like a tree and let the dead leaves drop.*

—RUMI

*Celebration of the Glory*

That brings us to the final stage, Glory or celebration. We have come to the stage of celebrating the event that occurred. We celebrate the life we had with the person we lost. Or we celebrate the lesson we learned from the event that occurred. It took me a long time to realize that I could celebrate what I had with my mom, my two horses, my three dogs, and my three cats. All of which I lost in a one-year period. I had lost my dad, my brother, grandparents, and aunt before that.

They were pretty much all my relatives that I knew. I know that I have other relatives out there. But none I am in contact with. My husband has relatives, and my stepdad had relatives. I am in contact with them. But I am the last of the biological relatives on my mother's side of the family. I was never in contact with the relatives on my dad's side of the family. I have a real sense that when I die, my side of the family will die. That branch on the tree will be gone. Not gone, but perhaps no further growth. I didn't have children, and neither did my brother.

## Sadness to Joy

I remember going through each of the states with the loss of each one of these people and animals in my life. I remember particularly when I spoke to a woman about the sadness I felt when I didn't buy a horse. The horse's name was La Vida. She was an Andalusian Arabian cross. She was seven years old and very well trained. I was looking for a horse after the sudden loss of my beloved Anastacia, a fourteen-year-old Andalusian mare. I rode La Vida and we had such a wonderful ride. I thought she was great. I got so excited, and then a few weeks later on the day she was to come home, she didn't pass her health check. She had bad hocks. And would soon be crippled by that condition.

I was devastated. I thought she was the perfect horse for me. I told a friend at a class I was attending, and she said, *Can you just be joyful for the time you had with her?* I kept thinking about what I didn't have instead of what I had had. Or more correctly what I had for a short time. It was then that I learned to *double down* on being grateful for what I did have and had experienced. I learned to translate that gratitude into many other experiences in my life.

I now celebrate the life I had with my mother. Even all the things I thought I particularly didn't like. But now I do. I love to use my ceramic meat defroster that she gave me, although when she gave it to me, I didn't think it was very useful. Now I use it every day, and I think of her when I do.

Do I miss those whom I have lost? Yes, I do. But even stronger than the sense of missing is the gratitude and the joy that I have for their having been in my life. There is a saying that *it is better to have loved and lost than to never have loved at all.* And that is true. Although it can take some time to go through the grief and pain that we feel. I recently replaced the cat loss a year ago with two lovely kittens rescued from the barn cats. And Ink Spot and Calvin bring Joy into our lives. When we celebrate the glory, we are in Absolute Gratitude. We are grateful for being grateful.

# Gratitude through Joy

*Butterfly*

Butterfly came by today again! The butterfly always heralds something important. It says to me that I should pay attention. Gratitude of, through, and by Joy is just sitting there waiting to be written. This is kind of the point of this book, *Absolute Joy.* I usually know what I'm going to say before I start writing. But I don't today. So, I start with Gratitude. I say, *Thank you, God, for the writing of this being so easy. Thank you for the flow of the words just pouring out on to the computer. Thank you for the wisdom, your wisdom that enables me to get it done.* And then I start writing and I am happy. Because it was easy. And then I am even more than happy because I am full of Joy.

*Process*

The above exercise in gratitude is a process. This process thanks God (Source) for the project already being done before we have even started it. I am thanking God for the positive outcome that I know is going to happen. Or already has. Being grateful for something that hasn't occurred helps to ensure the outcome. It makes life easier and puts us into Joy while we are accomplishing it. The writing of this piece is the perfect example of that.

Usually we think of this happening the other way around. We are happy or Joyful and it is conditional. We are happy because someone did something for us like the dishes or *(Good grief!)* like my husband dusted the house the other day because we were having company. His house cleaning made me happy and I was grateful. It is easy to be grateful for something that has happened. Or just happy that it happened. But I am suggesting that we give thanks for something before it happens as though it has already happened. Try it. You will find that the doing of it becomes much easier.

## Giving and Sharing

In this instance, happy and grateful seem to be the same thing. They almost are. But happy or joyful is internal and gratitude is external. What I mean by that is that we give gratitude out to someone else. Joy is something we feel. It is more internal. We can share Joy, and it radiates out from us even though we aren't intentionally sharing it. So, Joy is also given. Or more correctly, Joy is shared; and Gratitude is consciously given. Gratitude is a conscious act.

We can consciously share our Joy by telling a story about what happened. But that is more like being in the awareness of what is occurring than in actually consciously giving Joy. So, I think that gratitude is a conscious action, and Joy is shared.

## Gratitude through Joy

Gratitude through Joy. That is the easy way to look at it. We are happy about something and then we give thanks. It is the Joy we feel that puts us in the frame of mind to want to give thanks.

## Or Joy through Gratitude

It was my "Joy Experience," which I describe at the beginning of chapter 2, that took me from feeling gratitude to having the Joy experience. So, in that occurrence, the magic of gratitude led to Joy. Not the other way around. When I got up in the morning to do my Morning Prayer, I was so grateful for the morning, the sunrise, my coffee, and being alive and on the beach watching the sunrise in Bimini. Who wouldn't be! I felt extreme Gratitude. Then the heavens opened, and I had my Joy experience.

Sometimes Gratitude acts like magic to catapult us into Joy. I suggest you act with Gratitude often. Try this. Take seven complete deep breaths. With each breath you take, say, *Thank you for this breath. Thank you for this clean air.* Many people can't take deep breaths or don't have clean air. In addition to being in Gratitude, you will also feel peaceful and refreshed. It just may turn to Joy.

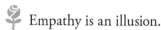 Empathy is an illusion.

# Gratitude through Love

### *The Attitude of Gratitude*

Gratitude and Love seem to be the same feeling. The energy is very close. Rhonda Byrne tells us in *The Secret* that the ancient texts sometimes equated Love and Gratitude. I think that Love is an energy that contains all things. I think that Gratitude is a giving. It has more movement as an energy. It is also an aspect of Love

When we go through the stages of Gratitude, we first allow something. This means that we don't resist something. Then we accept it. That acceptance is a little further down the path toward Gratitude. Then we feel Gratitude toward what has happened. There is also a next step and that is celebration. Joy happens somewhere between Gratitude and celebration. All of these attitudes that contain an energy are on a path that is a continuum.

### *Love Flows Gratitude*

When we love something with a human kind of love, we have a very warm energy in our hearts. We can't help but feel Gratitude for its existence. We look at something we love, like a puppy or a rose bush in bloom. We smile and a flood of emotion flows through us and sometimes we remember to say, *Thank you for being in my life.* Gratitude is giving and then we receive back an even greater rush of energy. God is saying, *And thank you for being in my life!*

Love as a human experience is sometimes seen that way also. As a giving and as a receiving. But I choose to define it as the energy of all things. And therefore, Love can't be given or received. It just is. Everywhere. When we happen to notice it, we feel Gratitude.

## Gratitude through Abundance

How could we not be grateful for the infinite abundance of all that is? Do we think that there is too much or that we are too small in such a large Universe? Gratitude is the right direction for our energy to flow. When we recognize that we live in an abundant Universe that is infinite, we can sometimes feel overwhelmed or lost. We could also or instead feel grateful, grateful that we are able to choose from an infinite buffet.

 We cannot be grateful and overwhelmed at the same time.

*Overwhelm: Re-entry Culture Shock*

I can remember coming back from living overseas in the Peace Corps. I had lived on an island in the Pacific that was a quarter of a mile wide by three quarters of a mile long. We had a very limited choice of food. Bananas, breadfruit, coconut, limes, and a wide variety of seafood. As well as some food that came in on the field trip ship every six weeks. We lived on two similar islands within the same atoll for two years.

When we came home, I went into a grocery store in the US, and walked down the aisles. I looked at the cereal choices. I couldn't choose. There were way too many choices. *Why did Americans need so many cereal choices?* I walked out of the grocery store buying nothing. I had been overwhelmed.

I was not grateful for the choices. I was overwhelmed. Over time I became used to the variety we have in our grocery stores. And now I even travel forty-five minutes away to go to a bigger store because they have more variety than the store in the small town where I live. I have become accustomed to the large variety of selections. I could judge this as a good or bad thing depending on whether or not I believe that it is wasteful and unnecessary. If we live in a world with limited resources, we shouldn't be wasteful. Being wasteful is not being a good steward of the earth.

*Stewardship*

The abundance of the Universe is not the same as the abundance of the planet earth, although we could apply the same rules of energy and the law of intention to the planet earth as we do to the universe. We also need to see the planet as infinitely wealthy and healthy. And we need to not bury our heads in the sand hiding, but rather participate in the healing of the earth. We should ask it what it needs and would like to see from us. Ask it how we can contribute to its healing of itself.

Yes. There is infinite abundance. But we also need to be good stewards of the land. Or this magnificent earth will die as an experiment in humanity that didn't work.

Gratitude is part of the equation. Gratitude for the earth and its ability to heal itself. Acceptance for what is and gratitude for that abundance also.

Thank the Universe for its infinite buffet of experiences. For the endless sunrises and exquisite oceans and infinite stars in the sky. For all the trees and plants and flowers, and the infinite opportunities to experience them all. Thank the Universe for the infinite abundance that is! And at the same time be a good steward of the earth.

## Gratitude through Peace

How could we not be grateful for a moment of quiet and a place where there is no struggle? Or do we not see that it exists? When we see that the place of Peace exists, we naturally step into it. In that place of Peace, Gratitude flows. Sometimes we say, *I thank God for this quiet. For this moment.* We can also intentionally create more Gratitude by creating more peaceful moments. When we choose Peace, we are aligned with an aspect of God or the Universe. We choose Peace by letting go of struggle and choosing easy. Ask about any decision you have to make, *What is the easiest way to do this? What is the best easy way?* Choose that way. And be grateful for the easy path.

# Gratitude through Magic

*Catalyst*

How could we not be in Gratitude for the mysterious and inexplicable world that we live in? The more grateful we are for the Magic we see around us, the more Magic we see. Gratitude is the catalyst for many things including magic. But is magic a catalyst for gratitude? Of course, the reverse is true. Magic might show up, in fact it does, even if we aren't grateful. But often we don't see it. We don't notice the magic that is around us constantly. We don't notice the signs of magic. The birds that show up or the phone call or the right book or the person who calls. Just when we need them to. We don't notice those things. When we do notice them and thank the Universe for them showing up, we get even more. And we notice even more.

*Mysterious*

We live in a mysterious and inexplicable world. Science tries to explain it, and it does a good job for many useful things. Like creating medicine and sending a man to the moon. Science is good for that. But it can't really explain the mysterious wonder that is the Universe. Mystery is the realm of Magic. The more we accept it as mysterious, the more we can be grateful for that mystery. And the more mystery will show up. Gratitude begets Magic begets Gratitude. Science would not like that statement. It would see it as circular reasoning. But it isn't reasoning at all. It's Gratitude through Magic.

 If you are not affirming it, you are denying it in silence.

# Gratitude through Intention

*Practice Gratitude*

We intend Gratitude by practicing it. We could take all the practices of gratitude and tell ourselves that we should and will do them every day.

We could break them down and say, *I will do this one on Monday and this one on Tuesday.* Those are ways we can get ourselves to practice gratitude.

### Heart Centered

Also, it matters what is in our hearts as we do this. To practice without Gratitude in our hearts is only good for creating habitual patterns. A habit is a good thing to create. Especially if it is a good habit. A good habit will eventually lead to real gratitude practiced daily. Gratitude can be seen as conditional. Something happens and we are grateful for it. But what if we are grateful for whatever happens? What if we are grateful for the experience of what is happening? That would be closer to unconditional Gratitude. Practice makes perfect they say. And perfect practice is even better. Perfect practice is practicing Gratitude no matter what. Giving Gratitude for all that shows up. If you are not giving Gratitude, then you are ungrateful. You are ungrateful in your silence.

## Gratitude through Divine Perfection

### Shifts in Time and Space

I gazed out my dining room French door this morning. I let my eyes relax.

> The room immediately shifts. The inside is dark and the outside is light. There is no color. Except for our red Ford truck parked in the distance out by the barn. Everything is brown or white this time of the year. There is generally no color or smell, and very few sounds. Everything is a brownish grey. No color. Inside is dark and outside somewhat lighter. Everything has light surrounding it. Everything is vibrating.
> I let my vision go double. It is hard to remain in that double vision. But I relax into it. So, there are two lines of dividers that are the grilles in the French door. The double lines shift back and forth. It takes me some time to relax into being in the world of doubles. Soon I am relaxed and even if I blink and breathe, the double images remain.

*Then there is a shift. And everything starts to move. Almost like heat evaporating off a hot sidewalk. The world shifts. Nothing is solid. There is no depth perception because space is disappearing.*

Then my mind brings me back. I think that time will disappear also when space disappears. Because if you don't have space, then you don't have time. I think that it is easier to shift space than to shift time. But then I am a spatial person. I am visual. So, I think that is okay. I can shift time by shifting space. That's easy.

## Healing in Time and Space

I think about a past incident where I used my energy to heal a woman who didn't want to be healed. She had been complaining about her sinuses at dinner, and I reached over above her head and pulled out two dark plugs that were floating in space above her. I thought I was helping since I do that for myself all the time. She got angry and said she didn't want anybody doing anything to her. I apologized. But I didn't put them back. They had already been dissolved by the energy around us. It didn't matter. Because she drew them back in herself. She was comfortable with her pain. I was reminded to never help a person unless they ask for it.

Sometimes I am too eager to jump in to help. But people see it as intrusive and it is. Even though I also believe that we don't really have to do anything, and people will be helped by the high energy of our presence.

I write about this because this morning I played with this incident in time and space. I created a different outcome where my intrusion never happened. And if I let it go, it didn't. I didn't entirely let it go because I just learned something from it. I do let go of any judgement I have around it. We let go of our judgement by letting go of the story.

What is important about the story in this moment is the ability to change past events in space and time. Do we really need to change them? No. We don't need to change them because they are in Divine Perfection. But I think that changing them is fun. So, I do.

## *Gratitude, Butterflies, and What's Next?*

I drew a card from my Morning Prayer card deck. It was Gratitude. The picture was a butterfly. The card said, *Butterfly flutters by*. During this time of the winter, there are no butterflies. But the card reminds me that the butterflies herald in something that I am to be aware of. It seems the butterfly appears when I need to pay attention. So, this card appears because I need to pay attention. What am I paying attention to? I think *Gratitude.*

Gratitude has been part of my attention for many years. A couple of months back I consciously practiced gratitude every day for three months. I used Rhonda Byrne's twenty-eight-day gratitude practices from her book, *The Magic*. Many of those practices have stuck with me. I always start my Morning Prayer with gratitude. I start my day with *I wonder what magical, wonderful thing will happen today*. When I get in the shower, I am reminded to be thankful for the hot shower. I carry a gratitude rock in my back pocket. It is a very flat, heart-shaped agate. At night when I go to sleep, I take out my pink quartz, heart-shaped rock that my friend Leslie gave me. Every night I ask what was the best thing that happened today, and I recount all the good things that I am grateful for and I pick one to be the best. Many of these activities I have done for years. In addition, for three months I added the exercises that Rhonda Byrne wrote about in her book.

I believe that all magic starts with gratitude. My pivotal Joy experience that occurred in 2015 was kicked off by Gratitude. So, I am very much believe in the power of expressing gratitude. I think that you can't express too much gratitude.

But I don't think that the card was about remembering Gratitude as much as it is about a butterfly asking me to pay attention. Butterflies appear when they need to. And since this is winter, they appeared in a card. Something is about to occur. I will let you know when I recognize it.

I walked out to the mailbox after feeding the horses this morning. As I walked, I asked what should I notice? I heard: *Everything. Notice everything! Ah. I should be grateful for the divine perfection of everything!* I just recognized it.

# Gratitude through Purpose

## *The Glory*

This morning I heard the word, *Glory*. And then I drew a card from the Morning prayer Card deck, and it was *Wisdom*, not *Glory*. I looked at the card for *Glory*. The animal was Rooster. The card said, *Rooster crows at the break of dawn*. I wondered why I chose Rooster for that card. He isn't a very majestic animal. Not like a peacock. Certainly, a peacock is so much more glorious. But no. Glory isn't about beauty. It's about the rooster crowing at the break of dawn, which is about the Glory. The break of dawn is one of the most Glorious events. The colors take your breath away, and then we are given another day. The rooster tells us to watch and be thankful and to sit in the Glory that is the break of a new day. That is why he anchors the Glory card.

## *Wisdom*

And what is Wisdom? I look at the card for wisdom. The picture is of a sequoia. The card says *Sequoia listens*. Listening is certainly good advice. It is wise to listen.

I think about the Glory of the heavens. I see trumpets blaring and angels singing. It is certainly a place of Glory of God in the highest.

Then I think about the middle world, the earth where we live. What if every step and every breath were to step into the Glory of God? And I thought, *It already is*. We just don't notice it or see it that way. But the animals do. The sequoia listens. So does the maple tree out my dining room window. And the birds at the feeder. They all hear the constant singing of the Universe as it plays the song of life through them. We sing also. The life force of the Universe is playing its one song (uni-verse) through us.

I look at the lower world where the icons of all species live—Wolf, Bear, and Dolphin—as well as the magical creatures like Dragon and Fairy. Sometimes the worlds mix, and the fairies and dragons show up in this middle world or sometimes in the higher world, especially when we ride them and their energies there.

There is really no difference between the worlds because there is really no time or space. We just use the differences to separate them so that we can enter them and enjoy our journeys there.

Our Purpose is to celebrate what is, the Glory of what is, the Divine Perfection of what is. Our Purpose is to experience it all. And we get to choose. I choose to celebrate the Glory and I am grateful for the freedom of choice.

# Energy of Gratitude

What is the energy of Gratitude? It is a little like Love and a little like Joy. When we are joyful for something and when we love something, we are also grateful for it. So, the energy of Gratitude is a little bit contained in those energies. But just because we are grateful for something doesn't necessarily mean that we love it. But it's close. The best Gratitude is heartfelt. It comes through our heart.

## *Energy of Judgement*

When we are grateful in our mind or we think that we should be grateful, but we aren't really, then it isn't Gratitude. It is a judgment about how we should feel. Like when we receive a gift that we don't like, and we think we should be grateful anyway. That is the energy of judgment not the energy of Gratitude. Gratitude is from the heart. It comes from the same place as Joy and Love. That is why it can get mingled with those energies. That is not a bad thing. Sometimes it is just easier to love something than to be grateful for it.

## *Receiving Energy*

The difference is that gratitude has the energy of receiving in it. Love is just something that exudes out of us as does Joy. Gratitude is more conditional. I am grateful for this something that I have received. And I say thank you. Both Love and Joy are more unconditional. I don't receive my husband. But I Love him. I can also be grateful for him.

The more that you are grateful for the things in your life, the more they will show up. The energy of Gratitude is giving thanks. It is expressing *Thank you.* It is putting your hand on your heart and giving heartfelt thanks. Gratitude is both a receiving and a giving energy. When we are grateful for absolutely everything it becomes Love.

# Sacred Technologies of Absolute Gratitude

*Techniques for Gratitude through Gratitude*

1. **Resistance to an Event.** Say three times, *In the name of God and all that is light, I* (state your name) *let go of my resistance to this event.* (State what the event is.)
2. **Acceptance of an Event.** Say three times, *In the name of God and all that is light, I* (state your name) *accept this event.* (State what the event is.)
3. **Give Thanks for an Event.** Say three times, *In the name of God and all that is light, I* (state your name) *give thanks for this event.* (State what the event is.) *Thank you. Thank you. Thank you.*
4. **Celebrate an Event.** Say three times, *In the name of God and all that is light, I* (state your name) *celebrate the lessons I have learned. Thank you. Thank you. Thank you.* (Replace *lesson* with freedom or power or with whatever lesson you ad.)

*Techniques for Gratitude through Joy*

5. **Gratitude for Breath**. Take seven complete deep breaths. With each breath, say, *Thank you for this breath. Thank you for this clean air.*
6. **Joyful Condition.** Think of something you are joyful about. Give thanks for it. Say thank you three times.
7. **Gratitude for Easy.** When you begin a project. Thank the Universe for its successful outcome before you have even started. Say, *Thank you for this project being so easy and so successful.* Put it in your own words. And see how easy it becomes.

*Techniques for Gratitude through Abundance*

8. **Abundance Everywhere.** Say three times, *Thank you for the abundance that exists everywhere. Thank you. Thank you. Thank you.*
9. **Abundant Condition.** Say three times, *Thank you for the abundant* … (fill in the blank). *Thank you. Thank you. Thank you.*
10. **Abundant Experience.** Say three times, *Thank you for the abundance of the experiences that fill my day. Thank you. Thank you. Thank you.*

*Techniques for Gratitude through Peace*

11. **Easy.** Ask what is the best and easiest way to do this? Listen for the answer.
12. **Easy life.** *I* (state your name) *accept that my life is easy.*
13. **Gratitude for Ease.** *I* (state your name) *am grateful that my life is easy. Thank you, thank you, thank you.*

*Techniques: for Gratitude through Purpose*

14. **Resistance to Glory.** Say three times, *In the name of God and all that is light, I* (state your name) *let go of my resistance to the Glory of God (the Universe).*
15. **Accept Glory.** Say three times, *In the name of God and all that is light, I* (state your name) *accept the Glory of God.*
16. **Step into Glory.** Say three times, *In the name of God and all that is light, I* (state your name) *step into the glory of God in all my being and doing.*
17. **Celebrate Glory.** Say three times, *In the name of God and all that is light, I* (state your name) *celebrate the Glory of God in my "beauty."* (Replace *beauty* with whatever you are resisting.)
18. **Wisdom.** Listen. Be in silence for one hour, half a day, or a full day. Do not speak. Just listen. Listen to the plants and animals. Listen to the silence. Do this as often as you can.

CHAPTER 8

# ABSOLUTE MAGIC

 Reading is magic. The stories arrive and depart with the wind.

## Magic of Magic

*Dream: The Magic House*

> *I am having a get-together at my magic house. I am a teacher and have my students over. We tour through the house and then we go outside. Everywhere we look there is something magical. I see magic rocks on a beach. Some people are outside cordoned off. They stand behind a yellow tape like they do in a murder scene in a movie. Some Zombies walk by. But they aren't ghoulish, just pale and dead looking. I pay them no attention in the same way that I don't pay them any attention in my waking life. Then a student comes by on a flying carpet. I think that the carpet should be more like a stiff metal sheet so that it won't flap in the wind as one soars around on it.*
>
> *Silly me to think that a magic carpet needs to be any different. It's magic after all, and it can be anything it wishes. Then I think that it should have a glass bubble on the top of it to protect the passengers from any flying debris from going fast or from flying too high with no oxygen. Again, I think silly me for thinking a magic carpet needs anything. It's magic!*

## *Magic of Presence*

The Magic of Presence and the Presence of Magic. What is it that is magical? Magic is something that happens, which we can't explain. One might say, *That is almost everything.* Science tries to explain everything. And it can't. Quantum physics would say that magic is closer to the explanations than scientific testing is, because of the influence of the observer on what is observed. This leads to what some call *biocentrism.* Biocentrism is a universe that is created by the observer.

I like to call that creation, *Magic.* I call it that because I believe I can wave "my magic want" at the universe and have it manifested. It actually goes beyond the *waving of the want* explanation. I don't wave my *want* because I have let go of my *want* and turned it into the energy of *having* and then I turn that *having* energy into *gratitude.* And then I turn that gratitude energy into *Joy.* And turn that Joy into celebrating what has just occurred. That process is my *magic want waving.* That is how I wave it at the Universe. And then I look around and say, *What's next?* Yes. I am celebrating what has already occurred and already is at this moment.

## *Presence*

Presence is being in the present moment. Not thinking about the past. Not letting the past define you. Or not worrying about or even looking forward to the future. Presence is being in this moment. We are here and now. Presence is placing us in time and space. We are not affected by the stories of our past. The stories that tell us *I am not good enough* and *I am not worried about the future.* They ask, *What if I fail at something?* and they make me wonder whether something does or doesn't happen. In this moment we are safe. We are safe because we are here.

From this place of presence, we make a choice about what we want to do, say, or be. And then the next moment happens and the next. We are in a continuous string of present moments. Continuously choosing. *That's exhausting,* you might think. To continuously choose. It isn't.

We can let our heart take over the choosing, and then we allow our mind to think about whatever it wants to think about, and we don't pay it any attention. We just notice that it is thinking about this or that. Often,

I give my mind something to do. *Here, think about this for a while,* I tell it. And off it goes. I give it a useful task. Like *What shall I write about in my next blog? Or Who should I vote for in the next election?* So, it is doing something. But I may or may not pay attention to it.

I'm not paying that much attention to it because I am not writing or voting from my mind. I am doing those things from my heart. And then when I vote it happens from my heart-mind. I bring my mind down into my heart, and then I act.

## Presence of Magic

Magic appears. Presence is always waiting. It is always here. It is a continuous string of *now heres*. And then seemingly out of nothing (nowhere) something appears. Isn't it funny that *nowhere* and *now here* are really the same? What appears might be something we consider magical, like a unicorn or a dragon, or it just might be the next candidate for president. He/she could just seem to appear out of nowhere.

## Chores and Magic

This morning my husband John told me about a dream he had about his mother and father. His mother was in the basement folding the laundry while dinner was up on the stove getting cold but having been made. She wanted to go upstairs to have dinner, but she had to finish the laundry first. She was frazzled. John, being the consummate fixer, was trying to arrange others in the family to do the chores so that she wasn't so fried.

As John slept, this morning, I woke up and came down the stairs. I was thinking about the household chores. John has been through three surgeries in the last couple of years and I have assumed many if not all of his chores. Slowly the chores have been going back to him as he recovers.

I was rationalizing that I feed the horses in the morning because I get up first. He feeds them at night because I go to bed early. I cook dinner and he does the grocery shopping. I do the dishes and he takes the garbage out. What we do in terms of chores is not equally doing the same chores, but we do the chores that each likes to do the most and the ones that we don't seem to hate doing. I hate driving the tractor and climbing into the hay mound. He does that. He hates mowing the lawn, but I love mowing the lawn. I love weeding the garden. We both find what we like doing, and we do that. Sorry—nobody likes dusting. We don't.

So, what does this have to do with Magic and Presence? Go back to the opening statements about both of us. As he was dreaming about the chores of his mother's household, I was thinking about our household, and wondering about the equity of the chores. Why was it we were both considering the same question at the same time? In his dream, John was trying to get his brothers to help his mother out. I was considering whether I needed John to help me more.

### Who Is Thinking?

Was it his thought that I was listening to from the *ether* or was it my thoughts that he was hearing while dreaming? Does the answer even matter? John and I are very connected. We have been married for fifty-plus years. So, we are very attuned to each other. But all people are really connected. It is just that when we are together for a long period of time, we notice it more.

When we have a thought, is it our own or is it someone else's thought? Does it matter? It matters if we believe that it is our own when it isn't. Did we choose to have it? Whether it is our own or someone else's, do we wish to have it? Do we wish to continue thinking it? Thoughts come up, and we can decide to focus on them or we can let them go and then choose what we do want to think about. When we choose it, it is our thought.

The Universe notices where we put our attention and intention. Attention goes first, and then our intention follows because that is where we have decided to put our focus. The Universe reacts and says, *Oh. That is where you want to go. Okay. Here it is and even more.*

That is the Magic of the Universe. In the present moment and only the present moment we can influence this. We notice and act in the present moment. What we see around us seems to pop up of nowhere. And guess what, it has. It's Magic. It is the Absolute Magic of the present moment that we continue to choose.

# Magic through Joy

This morning's sunrise was magnificent. A bright polished copper sun rising above the "V" formed by the roof of the stable building meeting the slope of the roof of the granary building. The polished copper ball peeked over the "V" in front of a pastel, water-colored, painted pink and lavender sky. The sight took my breath away as I began my Morning Prayer with gratitude. It's so easy to feel grateful when that sight is in front of you. I know that my gratitude is heartfelt when tears come to my eyes.

After feeling gratitude I wondered what aspect of God would come to me today. It was *Healing*. I wasn't sure of the word until after the vison and then I asked, *What is my word for today?* Duh. It was Healing.

*Vision: Fairytale Healing*

> *There is a person in front of me. I zip him open down the front of his body. And then I take out the frogs. There are six of them. Funny, I think. To take out frogs. Why frogs? Frogs are funny. They aren't bad.*
>
> *The frogs hop around and then they dissipate as they go out into the universe. I zip the person back up. I am not aware whether it is a man or woman. It doesn't seem to be either.*
>
> *Then I think. Oops! I should put something back in to take up the space of the frogs. I shouldn't leave the person hollow. So, I unzip the person again and pour flowing Joy inside from a watering can. I simply fill him up with Joy. Then I zip him back up.*
>
> *I think that I probably didn't have to remove the frogs. I could just transform them into Joy. Frogs are so full of laughter anyway. But most people want the things distressing them to be removed. The mind thinks that we have to remove these things. So, I am appeasing the mind when I do this kind of psychic surgery. But it isn't really necessary. We can simply transform the energy where it is and move on.*

*What does it Mean?*

Funny, I thought of turning frogs into princes. Isn't that a metaphor? So, the person in front of me was definitely a man. I was simply turning his frogs into princes. So, was it the kiss of Love? It was the Magic of Joy. I poured in Joy water. Joy is an aspect of Love.

The subtitle of my second book, *Beyond Joy: A Journey into Freedom, Wisdom, Power, and Wellbeing*, says, "What if your life were a fairy tale waiting to be written by you?" I guess it is.

 When you recognize your value, your gifts wake up.

## Magic through Love

When we experience Love, does our world magically change? Yes, it does. Look at the young couple who are in Love. Their sense of time and whatever is happening around them is different. They behave differently. They are so into each other that they are almost unaware of the world around them. That awareness changes over time, and so does their total absorption in each other. So why does this happen? And what does Love have to do with Magic?

Our health is better when we are in love. Our decisions are easier. But not necessarily better. I would like to think that people in love make better decisions. But I don't think that. What is Magic? Magic is the happening of the unexplainable.

*Magic Happens*

I do think that people who stand in Love with their awareness and listen to their hearts make better decisions. Sometimes young people in love are blinded by their love in their decision-making. So, it isn't about "being in love." It's about standing in Love with awareness. That is to say, putting our hearts into our minds and acting from that place. When we have awareness and we look around, what do we see? Things happen that we can't explain. Magical things happen.

*Magical Gifts*

When we recognize our value. When we love ourselves and when we love another, all of our gifts wake up. What do I mean by that? I mean that we are more aware, clearer, more powerful, more loving, more peaceful, more at ease, more …. Fill in the blank with your own gift. All of our gifts appear as if they were Magic. And that is exactly what they are, magical gifts.

## Magic through Abundance

*Infinite Possibility*

The possibility of infinite Abundance sets the stage for Magic. When we have a stage for infinite possibility, there is nothing that cannot happen. Now that's a stage! And then it comes into being.

We don't know how or why or when, except we know the timing when we see it happen. If we had limitation in the world, then magic couldn't happen, or magic would have rules. I think that we would call that science. Science happens by rules. Rules are a good thing. We can send a man to the moon by those rules and we can cure diseases. But what if we could also achieve those things by Magic?

*No Limitations*

What if we could beam a person to the moon? And what if he could then breathe there? Or what if we could cure disease by Magic or if diseases magically didn't even exist?

Magic has no rules or limitations. It is the result of a limitless and infinite Universe. Rules try to limit a limitless Universe. Magic is how the Universe truly functions. We only paint it with the color of science. We explain it and then we expect it to behave that way. And it does. Until it doesn't. And then we say that it is Magic. Magic is born thorough Abundance. Through the limitless infinite.

# Magic through Peace

*Power Over*

There is a difference between *power of* and *power over*. Bullies have power over. They are stronger or smarter, and they use that to bully another person. It can be physical bullying or mental bullying. A person who uses his intellect to blast another in a conversation is also bullying. A woman who uses her beauty to dominate another is also bullying. A young person who demeans another one on the internet is bullying. Bullying is not true power. It is power over. There is no Magic in power over.

The person who claims to be victimized or who self-deprecates is also using a form of power over. Or maybe we should call it *power under*. The person who says, *Poor me. I didn't have the same advantage.* Or *I'm too disabled to ….* I'm not talking about the people who were really victimized or who are disabled. I'm talking about the people who have defined themselves and their lives around a perceived victimhood or disability. They have claimed this victim status to exert power over another. It is the power of a *poor me* receiving sympathy and mistaking that attention for love.

So, both self-deprecation and bullying are forms of power over. Having to be in control is also a form of power over. The person who has to always be in control of the situation is trying to have power over the situation. Having to get the last word in is a form of control. Contrast that behavior with the behavior of *power of.*

*Power Of*

True power is the power of …. *Power of* is the power of Love, Peace, and Joy. It is the power of all the aspects of God or conditions of the Universe. It includes the power of Magic. It's not that the power of Magic is a separate power. It is *the* power. Magic is the infinite power of the infinite Universe.

When we think of magic, we think of someone waving a magic wand at the condition around him, and it changes. We think that the wand waving is the magic.

But what if we wave Love at hate and the hate disappears? What is left? Love. What if we wave Peace at struggle? What is left? Peace. What if we wave Freedom at abuse? And freedom remains. What if we wave virtue at corruption? What remains? Virtue.

That is true Power, the power of. The Power of Peace, of Virtue, of Love, and of Freedom. These powers are not over another, but they do dissolve the negative emotion that is in their presence.

## Magic Condition of Peace

These powers seem magical and they are. Love is Magic, Peace is Magic. These conditions are Magic. If you wave them at their opposite condition, that condition vanishes. Does this mean that the child on the playground who is being bullied or the adult at work who is being bullied should not report it? Should they just offer Love? No. They should absolutely report the abuse. The abuse is wrong. Then they should step into the Peace that forgiveness gives. Forgiveness also brings its own power. Report. Forgive. Be at Peace and stand in the magical power of Freedom.

## Intellectual Bullying

I often experience intellectual bullying, when a very intelligent and well-educated person tries to command a conversation because they think that their intellectual brilliance puts them on the higher ground of right. People often have to defend that they are right. The ego doesn't want to be wrong. It has to be right no matter what. The *no matter what* sets the stage for bullying. In this case, intellectual bullying. It can be a war zone.

In this case, I'm not playing war. I say, *Okay. You win the battle*, and if I'm able, I walk away. Or I just say, *You are right.* I could also say something like, *That's interesting. I will have to give that some thought.* If I let go of having to be right, I can stand in Peace or Joy. True power is in Peace or Joy. Not in winning the battle.

But then you ask, *What if they are wrong?* You can state your opinion. But you don't have to defend it at all costs. It's the *at all costs* that makes you lose your power. State your opinion and be done with it.

125

The Magic is that some part of them heard you. They don't have to dig in to such a deep trench if they don't have to defend it. And then it is easier for them to climb out. Change comes more easily if we aren't entrenched in our belief systems. Allow them to be with their beliefs while you stand in your own power. Stand in the Magic, in the power of Peace.

## Magic through Intention

Magic happens whether we want it to or not. Whether we notice it or not. Whether we intend it or not. Sometimes when we wave our magic wand at something, it doesn't happen. Or at least it doesn't happen in the way that we want it to. Like my example of the shopping cart in chapter 2.

What happens is that our energy is directed by our attention. Our noticing. If we feel the need to wave our wand at something, then we feel that we need to change it. That it needs fixing or changing. We are not in allowance. If we were in allowance, we wouldn't need to wave our wand at it.

Co-Creation and Divine Perfection are already at work. So is Magic. It is already happening. We can notice that it is. We can encourage it even more. We can say *thank you* for what is occurring. That way the Universe knows that we want more of it. But we don't need to go into the energy of wanting to try to make it happen. The energy of wanting only gives us more wanting.

## Magic through Divine Perfection

*Belief in Magic*

I drew a card this morning from the Morning Prayer Card deck and it was *Magic*. It had a picture of a Unicorn. It said, *Unicorn appears*. Magic doesn't appear until you believe in it. It happens when children play make believe. Playing make believe is making our beliefs come true. I'm also reminded of the opposite. Not believing in something until it no longer exists. In the movie, *Merlin*, Merlin's final act to get rid of Morgan le Fay was to turn his back on her and to forget her, and to encourage all of the people around her to forget her. Then she ceased to exist. It worked because Magic only works if you believe in it.

## Intention

Belief really isn't magic—it is the power of intention directed by our beliefs and focused with our intent. It is held there by our will. To strengthen our magical ability, we need to strengthen our belief, our intention, and our will. We need to strengthen all three.

I recently had an experience in magic with fairies at a reunion at Rikka Zimmerman's house. It was a graduation ceremony for Rikka's Life Transformed Coaches. She was crowning each of her newly graduated coaches with a golden garland halo signifying their ability to be angels on earth in their coaching practices.

## The Rose Garden

The ceremony was held in a garden surrounded by hundreds of roses. Mostly tea roses but several other kinds also. All the roses were in various stages of blooming with white, red, yellow, and pink petals. So beautiful. Since roses are very special to me, I walked around and talked to several of them, praising them for their exquisite beauty. They praised me back.

The ceremony included two separate fairy elixirs that had a fruit juice base. I know that rose tinctures were in there, plus many other essences that were brewed by Peter May. Peter is a fire fighter and plant enthusiast. He is also an award-winning musician who plays music with plants that are hooked up to a machine that changes their vibration into song. I'm sure that the pinyon pine essence was also in there, because Peter is also known as "Pinyon Pine Peter." As he has a special connection to the pinyon pine, it is in most of his essences. Peter also played the "Music of the Rose." Or I should say that the rose played her own music and Peter accompanied her with a didgeridoo. The whole ceremony was quite magical in itself. We invited the Fairies to join us. But of course, they were already there.

*The Fairies*

> *I see them poking me and flittering at me on my shoulders. They kept poking me, kind of like, You're it! Chase me! Flit flitting and poking. Then I see thousands of them hovering over the fairy drinks that are waiting to be distributed. They seem to be sprinkling fairy dust in them. There are many other beings also sprinkling things into the drinks.*

We thank the fairies and other beings for their assistance. I thought about the flitting of the fairies and I wished that I too could flit like they do.

> *Well, maybe not flit, I think. But at least fly around. Maybe if I had wings on my feet like Mercury has, I could fly around like they do but slower. And then I lurch forward. It isn't so much of a lurch as something like the movement of the superhero Flash. I kind of flash forward a short space and then abruptly stop. Definitely not a flit. A surge forward and then a stop like I had hit a wall. Not particularly pleasant.*

I told someone about it later, and she asked if it was like being beamed up in the television series *Star Trek*. I said, *No. It was more like a flash forward with an abrupt stop.* Oh well. Be careful what you ask for. You just might get it.

I find the fairies to be tricksters. Always poking and prodding. They say, *Here I am. Look over here.*

Well, that is one kind of Magic. A fairy kind of magic. I prefer to see Magic as something that's slower, evolving, and beautiful. I tend to see everything as Magic, including being alive. If you want to have more Magic in your life, you have to see more Magic. If you want to see more Magic, you have to acknowledge the Magic that is already here.

One way to do this is to list all the magical occurrences or maybe cosmic coincidences that you have seen in your life. Then make a list of those you saw yesterday. Soon your lists will get bigger and bigger until you see everything as magical, which it is. Including being alive and breathing. Life in Divine Perfection is the true Magic.

Many scientists believe that the universe is expanding and will eventually contract. Is God just breathing in and out?

## Magic through Purpose

*The Truth*

Truth can be discovered in the magnificence of whatever we are looking at. This morning it was a glorious sunrise. I'm not sure that it rose to the level of Bliss, however. But I think that the Truth of Bliss can be found in the glow of the firefly. It can be found in things that glow and let out their light. The enlightened being standing in Bliss glows his light out to the world. But where is Truth in consciousness? What I am questioning is whether or not to let the consciousness of the group or the consciousness of collective humanity determine what the Truth is. Can a group consciousness determine what is Truth?

*The Becoming Universe*

I believe in an infinitely intelligent Force that created the God code of our DNA. As we evolve, we become increasingly more self-aware. Creating living organisms is just a way for the Universe to know itself and to evolve. The Universe is always becoming ….

If we create our own reality, then we create the Truth. But if we create it, can it really be the Truth? If the Universe has a greater Truth, then we should step into that. But I fear that I am only stepping into the truth of humanity. I'm not sure that I trust the consciousness of that group. Do I think that we will evolve? Do I think that we can align ourselves with the Force and intelligence of the Universe so that we can evolve?

 What if our purpose is to align with the purpose of the universe?

## *Adaptation and Survival*

We will not survive as a species if we don't adapt and evolve. The dinosaurs didn't. They went too far down a particular path that led to their extinction. I fear if we don't take better care of our planet, we will cause our own extinction. The news the other day reported that one third of the earth's animal species will be extinct if climate change goes unchecked. I taught Green Architecture for twenty years. And finally, now, some of the politicians are getting on the band wagon of sustainability. But not all, and not those who are in power.

I do believe that we change thinking with a critical mass of right thinking. That is called the Truth. That is also called voting the right candidates into office. But even if we don't do that, we can change the thinking of humanity with a ground swell of thought. Then the elected officials will have changed their thinking also. Like the hundred monkeys. So many monkeys think and act in a certain way, and then they all do. No inference intended between monkeys and politicians. But it is difficult not to see the similarities. I hope that we can make the right adaptive changes soon, and I hope that we can be the responsible stewards of our planet before it is too late.

## *The Magic of Laughter*

I choose not to create the reality that it is too late. I choose to create the reality that will change the thinking of all those who are in power and will ever be in power. I choose to live in that world. The truth is that we create our reality. I choose to create that reality.

Laughter is a harbinger of Truth. We need to laugh at ourselves. Laughter relieves us of the stress we are holding. While matters seem to be serious, if we laugh at ourselves, we can make better decisions. When we laugh, we are aligned with the Joyous flow of the Universe. We are more tapped into the divine consciousness, which is always laughing, not at us but with us. The Truth is a magnificent universe. With Infinite possibilities. Not just one possibility of an unsustainable and dying or, at the least, struggling planet. Instead, I choose to see it as an infinite planet with infinite possibilities.

Where does the Magic come in? It comes in with the mystery of it all. It comes in with the not knowing. It comes in with the acceptance of the magnificence without our knowing why or how or even what the event is that occurs.

*Magnificence Leads to Bliss.*

Where does that leave us? We can step into the Magnificence of it all, and then take even a further step. We can step into the Bliss of it all. We can shine our light out at the world because we are so filled with that light that it shines out from us no matter what.

Then what happens? The world steps into a little more alignment with the evolution that the Universe seeks. It seeks that evolution because it likes change. It wants to experience its own growth, and we are a part of that growth. We have free will so that we can experiment with change, and if that change is a good change, then we evolve. We have to adapt like the giraffes with their long necks. So, they evolve and survive, and we evolve and survive. And then the Universe gets to evolve and experience itself as it evolves. That is our Purpose—to evolve and experience the Magic of the Universe.

# Energy of Magic

This morning I decided to explore the energy of the chakras. What would happen if I tasted and smelled the seven chakras? What would that be like?

So, I start with the *root chakra*, the red one. It's where safety is stored. But what does it feel like? What does it smell and taste like? Maybe it's the color of a red rose. It smells like a rose. That makes sense because the rose is my pathway. The pathway of the rose. I like that, and I can smell and breathe in the color, taste, and smell of a deep red rose. The perfume is almost overwhelming.

Then I go to the *sacral chakra*. That's easy. It's orange. I take a deep breath and inhale the scent of an orange. I can taste the orange. The orange flavor floods my system. This is the creative chakra. I feel creativity flowing through me. I remember when I was working in Spain and all my clothes were orange. They called me *la chica naranja*.

I move to the *power chakra*. It's yellow. I wonder if I should stay with the citrus theme. I know it's easier for newbies to energy work to taste and smell a lemon. So, I go there. And yes, it works. But I am also drawn to butter. The smell of melted butter. What about the two of them together like lemon butter on a lobster. Yes. There is power there. I smell and taste the power of the lemon butter chakra.

I move to the *heart chakra*. I see a small glowing ball behind the heart. I know that it is green. But I also like pink. So What smell is green? For me, it is alfalfa. I salivate when I see a fresh mown field of alfalfa. But most people can't relate to that. So, what should I share? How about cucumber? It has a delicate and watery smell. I love cucumber water. So, I choose cucumber. The taste and smell of cucumber pervades my body.

I move to the *throat chakra*. This is the chakra of communication. A fruit would be blueberry. I try that out. It seems okay. It doesn't have strength until I think of hot bubbly blueberry pie. Then I know it works. I inhale hot blueberry pie.

I move to my *third eye chakra*. I see grapes and dark grape jelly. Particularly on toast. The sharp taste of homemade grape jelly gets my salivary glands juicing. I smell grape and I see grape.

So, what about the *crown chakra*? Of course, it's lavender. I smell lavender and I see the lace of a crocheted mat. Or maybe the undulations of a jelly fish. Although I'm not sure of the smell. It isn't lavender. I think of lavender fields. And I think of my friend Steffy who raises lavender. Yes, it's the lavender plant. I drink in the smell of a lavender field in bloom. But this isn't refined enough for bliss.

So, I reach up higher into a *gold chakra*. And the smell and taste of gold rains down through all the other chakras. Gold has a smell that permeates the back of my throat. I think that then I must also go lower than the bottom chakra and pull up the deep red damp smell of the earth. And I pull it all the way up and through the seven chakras to the gold chakra.

I run the gold energy down and the deep earth energy up. Up and down. Several times. I think about the fruit salad that I have created. Some people would say it's a rainbow. But I have created breakfast. And I say, *Good morning* to the day, already having had breakfast.

# Sacred Technologies of Absolute Magic

*Techniques for Magic through Magic*

1. **Bring your Heart into your Mind** or your mind into your heart. Both work. Do the one that seems easier to you. Breathe. Reach up into the highest vibration that you can find. Breathe. Reach down into the center of the earth. Breathe. Do this three times. Then find your center at your heart and bring your mind down into your heart. Let your awareness expand out from this state. You will find that you act in Peace.

2. **Watch your Mind.** Give your mind some activity to work on. Then let it go and don't think about it. Just watch it being busy.

3. **Presence.** Step into the present moment. Watch your breath. Take seven in and out breaths. Let go of any attachments to the past. Let go of any anxiety about the future. Look around you. What do you see right now? What is here? Now, what would you like to do?

*Techniques for Magic through Joy*

4. **Transform into Joy.** Say three times, *I now accept that anything in my life that isn't joyful can be transformed into Joy.*

5. **Magic of Transformation.** Say three times, *I now accept the Magic of transformation.*

*Techniques for Magic through Abundance*

6. **Infinitely Abundant.** Say, *I* (state your name) *believe in an infinitely abundant Universe.*

7. **Magical Universe.** Say, *I* (state your name) *believe that the Universe is magical.*

*Techniques for Magic through Peace*

8. **Breath of Peace.** Do seven-second breathing. Watch your breath. Breath in for seven seconds and out for seven seconds. Do this seven times. Then speak or take action.

9. **Decide to Be Right or to Be Peaceful.** The next time you enter into a confrontation, ask yourself, *Do I want to be right or do I want to be happy and in Peace?* State your opinion and then let it go.

10. **Power and Lightness.** Practice the exercise for power and lightness. Play with the lightness. Play with power. Combine the two. Send the lightest wisp of energy like a feather down into the earth and then up into the sky. How light a wisp can you send up into the sky and still feel its energy? Then reverse the process. Send the energy of an atomic bomb down into the earth and then up into the sky. How was that? Place the power of the atomic bomb into the lightness of the feather and then send it down into the earth and then up into the sky? How was that? Practice doing them separately and then together.

*Techniques for Magic through Divine Perfection*

11. **Past Magic.** List all the magical occurrences you have seen in your life.

12. **Past Cosmic Coincidences.** List all the cosmic coincidences you have seen in your life.

13. **Current Magic.** List all the magic that occurred yesterday.

14. **All Is Magic.** Say three times, *In the name of God and all that is light, by the law of divine grace, I* (state your name) *accept that all of life is Magic.*

*Techniques for Magic through Purpose*

15. **Step into Magnificence.** Say three times, *In the name of God and all that is light, by the law of divine grace, I* (state your name) *now choose to step into the magnificence of all that is.*

16. **Choose to Shine.** Say three times, *In the name of God and all that is light, by the law of divine grace, I* (state your name) *choose to shine forth my light.*

17. **Align with Love.** Say three times, *In the name of God and all that is light, by the law of divine grace, I* (state your name) *choose to align with the love of the Universe.*

18. **Conscious Intelligence.** Say three times, *In the name of God and all that is light, by the law of divine grace, I* (state your name) *choose to align with the conscious intelligence of the Universe.*

19. **Stand in Love and Cooperation.** Say three times, *In the name of God and all that is light, by the law of divine grace, I* (state your name) *choose to stand in love and cooperation with the Universe.*

20. **Already Done.** Say three times, *In the name of God and all that is light, by the law of divine grace, I* (state your name) *accept that it is already done.*

*Techniques for Magic through Energy*

21. **Seven Chakras.** Run through the seven chakras as explained in the chapter. Ask what color and what smell and what taste each one has for you.

22. **Experience the Energy of Magic.** Ask to be shown the energy of Magic. Say, *Universe will you show me what the energy of Magic looks like? Tastes like? Smells like? And feels like?*

# CHAPTER 9

# ABSOLUTE CO-CREATION

*He who works with his hands is a laborer. He who works
with his hands and his head is a craftsman. He who works
with his hands, his head, and his heart is an artist.*

—St. Francis of Assisi

## Co-Creation through Intention

*Dream: The Veil*

> *I am in a group. I levitate up. I am very high up in a room
> and I go into a corner. I spread my wings and I look down
> at the group. I speak to one of the members of the group. It
> is Virginia. I ask her if she would like to soar with me into
> the heavens. She says, Yes. We take off holding hands. Her
> own power accelerates our speed. I am amazed that I don't
> have to drag her along. I see a mist. I think about crossing
> through the veil. I think that it can be a challenge. But I tell
> myself, No. We will simply go through it. We do. I see light
> everywhere and then nothing. I wake up.*

We often speak of the veil as a curtain that we must pass through to
experience the dimension that is on the other side. People experience it as
many things, a mist, a mirage, and an energy field. When two different

energy fields come together there is a blending of energies where they touch. It could be like the shear that happens when hot and cold air come together. The hot air rises and the cold air falls, creating a shear. The air also rotates in opposite directions. All of these things happen when two different energies come together. When two people come together, we co-create. We also co-create with the Universe, whether we are aware of it or not.

## A Reflection

We get what we think about and what we feel. Our feelings are like rocket fuel. They intensify our thoughts. The Universe reflects back our thoughts with what surrounds us. The conditions of our life are in response to the direction and content of our thoughts and actions. Our actions are a result of our thoughts.

But how do we control our thoughts and direct them where we would like them to go? And are our thoughts even ours? Or are we simply thinking what is going on in the community or world around us? Can the community or friends around us influence what we are thinking? Or are we thinking what our parents taught us to think? We called that the socialization process when we were growing up. But it continues through our adult life and into the future. We have the ability to choose our thoughts. How? By redirecting them when we realize that they are not in alignment with what we truly want.

The energy of intention reflects our thoughts. We think *lack* and we see more lack. We think *not good enough* and we see more examples of *not good enough* around us. We *think poor health* and we see examples of that around us also.

So, isn't it time to realign our thoughts to what we do want instead of what we don't want? Even as we see what we don't want in front of us?

Intention is aligned through focused awareness. Direct it toward what you do want. How do we focus our awareness? By listening.

*Listen*

This morning I told myself to just listen. I always tell myself that near the end of my Morning Prayer, and then usually I hear a word. But my word today was *listen*. How do I listen to listening? I thought about communication. I'm not very clairaudient. I am more clairsentient, clairvoyant, and claircognizant. I am always reaching into another vibrational frequency and seeing a vision or simply knowing the answer.

I frequently do the exercise where I bring my mind down into my heart. I call it my heart-mind. I don't often differentiate the two. So, I also combine clairsentience with claircognizance. I don't really differentiate the two. I also don't care how I get the information, as long as I get it.

How do I reach into another vibrational frequency? First, I notice that it's there. Then I say, *Hello. Who and what are you?* Then I step into that space or I reach out with my knowing as if it were a finger into that space. Since my mind is almost always connected to my heart, there is a bit of feeling into it going on also. Then *Boom*. There is a vision of something or a simple knowing that I really already knew that information in my mind. Rarely do I hear words. But I certainly know them.

*Communication*

There are many forms of communication. We communicate with other people, the natural world, and ourself. We also communicate with the Universe. And all those things communicate with us. We simply need to notice the communication we are receiving constantly. Noticing is also a form of communication.

 The universe doesn't hear words, just the
vibration of the intention of the words.

The universe speaks first, and we listen. The Universe is always speaking and showing us. It says. *Look at me here and how about over here? Will you listen to me now? And How about now?* Of course, we can't listen and be talking at the same time.

We need to build our communication skills in order to converse with the Universe. Communication is not just the skill of talking. Communication includes the skills of seeing, listening, knowing, feeling, and noticing what is happening around you. One way to do this is to *Ground* before you step into the higher energies of feeling and knowing.

Co-Creation requires us to communicate. The more accurately we communicate the better. Muddled communication is also communication. But do you really want to create a muddled world? So is silence a communication. Want to Co-Create better? Learn to communicate better.

## Co-Creation through Joy

*Wisdom and Grace*

This morning's *Morning Prayer Cards* were Co-Creation, Wisdom, and Grace. I interpreted them to be Co-Creation through the Wisdom of Grace. I interpret Grace to be sweetness. I interpret Wisdom to be listening. It is the wisdom of the sequoia tree standing in silence and listening. It is the Grace of the bear in spreading his sweetness. And what do we Co-Create from that place?

I look around and there is infinite possibility. So, what would give me Joy? That is the question that I need to ask. That is what I choose. What would bring the world Joy? It would give me Joy to bring the world Joy. I have been called many things, a dream weaver, a weaver of worlds, a joy magnet, a Life Transformed coach, horse woman, architect, wife, author, writer, teacher, and speaker. But never a world bringer.

*World Bringer*

Maybe that is what I should be called, a World Bringer. I like that, a world bringer. And what world is it that I am bringing? I hope to bring a world of Joy. But also all those other aspects and conditions of Love that I have written about: Peace, Healing, Abundance, Harmony Grace, Freedom, Power, and so on. I have identified thirty aspects, conditions, and tools. I hope to bring into the world all the conditions, tools, and aspects of God.

It's not that I'm really bringing them in. They are already here. It is that I am removing the veil between humanity and those conditions so that humanity can see them better, can see that they are already here.

Sometimes we see that veil as blocks to our abundance or blocks to our health. And it does block us. But it is more that we are blocking ourselves from seeing what is already in front of us.

We have conditioned ourselves to not see what is in front of us. We need to change that conditioning. Our conditioning is rooted in fear of what we don't know or don't understand.

We need to let go of that fear, and offer kindness to ourselves and others instead.

### Power in Kindness

There is power in sweetness. I have never seen myself as sweet. In the past, I would have chosen power and strength for myself, like the kind of power Wonder Woman has. I would not have chosen being sweet. But now I realize that there is great power in sweetness. I would also call it kindness. A simple act of kindness can change the day of a person and sometimes his life. I believe that kindness could also change the direction and path of a nation.

What if we change how we dealt with immigrants at the border? We need to. How can we put children in cages? Or anybody for that matter? How can we put adults seeking asylum in cages? That is not kindness. Yes, we need to screen people so that we are safe. But we don't need to put people in cages. Kindness is not a weakness; it does not diminish us. It empowers us. And it empowers the other human being on its receiving end.

### Respect

Kindness is not a handout. It is mutual respect. It is respect for the other person and respect for ourselves. If we don't respect ourselves, we certainly can't respect the other person. With mutual respect comes empowerment. With empowerment comes nation building with the integration of the immigrants and others into our society. Respect is at the heart of nation building.

The same goes for those already here. It goes for our friends and family. If we show kindness and respect, we will be able to also be kinder to ourselves and show ourselves the same respect.

And then maybe we can be kind to our nation, and also respect it. Yes, we have made some mistakes. But we can learn from them and then we can move on.

### Co-Creation and Joy

So, is the right term the *Joy of Co-Creation*? Or is it the *Co-Creation of Joy*? Or does it even matter? I drew the Co-Creation card first. So how do we co-create Joy? We choose it. And we align with the Joy we see in the Universe. We look for Joy. How many instances of happiness or Joy can we see? What color is it? For me it is pink.

Yesterday was Valentine's Day and my husband gave me six roses. Five were pink and one was red. They were beautiful. Roses are especially beautiful to me. I use them to define the path I choose to stop and smell. So, there might as well be something as sweet smelling as the rose. The rose sings to me and smiles at me. The rose brings Joy into my life and I choose to see it and to follow my rose-petal-strewn path that I have Co-Created. And that is how you Co-Create your way into Joy. Align with your path, and Co-Create it with the Universe.

 It is a Yes to me.

## Co-Creation through Love

### Unconditional Love

Since everything is an aspect of Love, Co-Creation through Love is a given. Given by whom? Given by the Universe, of course. So, when I write about Co-Creation through Love, I mean the human kind of love we feel for one another in its highest sense. The unconditional love a mother feels for her children or her children feel for her.

When we stand in Love, we are in the best place to make all decisions. We are in the best place to take action. When we are standing in Love, we have the most clarity. Clarity does not come from the mind. It comes from joining the mind to the heart. Our higher self knows how we should act. But sometimes our mind doesn't let us hear our higher self.

*The Mind*

Our minds tell us to make lists and set goals. These are not bad things. But they are insufficient in making decisions and acting upon them. When we act, we are making a decision. And when we don't act, we are still making a decision. The best way to make a decision is to join our hearts to our minds and then act.

We are always Co-creating whether we are acting or not. The Universe is continuously offering us options to do something. To have an experience. The Universe is expanding and evolving into something else. We are expanding and evolving with it. It is expanding and evolving through our experiences. We can align and make our life easier with our alignment. Or we can struggle and try to go against it. We can co-create easily, or we can choose to struggle. Remember not choosing is also a choice.

*Align with Love*

Love is all there is. The Universe is Love. It accepts all things and loves us by giving us the freedom of choice. Love is total acceptance. But certain decisions will align and continue to grow and evolve, and others won't. They will cease to exist. Alignment with love—both the human kind and the universal kind, which is total acceptance—fosters evolution.

Creation of all kinds happens through Love. The Universe doesn't understand *no*. It only understands *yes*. *Yes* is the acceptance factor. *No* doesn't even really exist. To create we have to say *yes*. To Co-Create we have to say *yes* to the Universe. It is *yes* to the universe and *yes* to me.

## Co-Creation through Abundance

Does Abundance itself foster Co-Creation? It does if its infinite nature gets us up off the couch and makes us do something. It does if the excitement of having infinite possibilities at our disposal will get us moving and invigorated. How can having whatever we want at our fingertips or maybe *mind tips* not excite us?

But how do we choose what to Co-Create? We could choose whatever is fun and easy or we could bring in purpose and say whatever is aligned with the highest good of all. Or whatever makes my heart sing and would serve others at the same time. What in the realm of infinite possibilities would do that? Then we choose and the Universe aligns with our choice.

Or you could choose to do what your parents taught you or your teachers told you or the media tells you or your friends tell you or what makes you the most money. The Universe will support you in those things also, and you have infinite support to do those things. But you will struggle more and work harder to do those things. Why not take the easy and fun path of aligning with your purpose and the purpose of the Universe? You Co-Create either way.

## Co-Creation through Peace

*Multiple Realities*

Multiple realities are separated from each other in a similar way. Some people see heaven on earth happening in the exact same place where we are standing. Only it occurs in a different reality. One accesses that reality by stepping into the other. One usually experiences a veil of some kind. This is the energy where the two dimensions have mingled together somewhat. One can get lost in that space, and it can be confusing because neither reality is totally present. It is the focus of one's intention that allows us to step through the veil.

*Portal of Peace*

Sometimes there are portals. These can be places of power where the energies of the earth are aligned just right to access the portals. They can also be portals of our own making through meditation and energy practices. Or sometimes incidents of extreme stress or tiredness can induce them. And sometimes the experience of Peace and Joy can open them. Stand in Peace. Then walk through the portal.

And what do we find on the other side? I find the awareness of Co-Creation and infinite possibility. We find what we expect to find. What we imagine we will find. We find what we intend to find.

# Co-Creation through Magic

*Already Done Hasn't Really Happened Yet*

I think, therefore, I am. Yes. And I think, therefore, it is. We are well acquainted with the idea that our minds create our reality. Especially when the reality has something to do with beliefs and feelings about an event. We are also well aware of the ability to change our beliefs and feelings, and then we can change the events in our lives.

We are changing the description or the story around the event. When the description around the event changes, we say that it never really happened. But we are really changing our perception about what occurred. How we see an event is colored by our viewpoint. Another person sees the event differently. A good example was the impeachment hearings of President Donald Trump. Two sides, two viewpoints, and one event. But what if the event never did occur? Then what are talking about?

*Retrocausality*

I was reading *Beyond Biocentrism* by Robert Lanza, and I learned a new word, *retrocausality*. *Retrocausality* is when an observer in the present causes something to happen in the past. The author gave the example of something happening billions of years ago like a quasar light bending around a galaxy because it really was the shortest route due to the pull of the galaxy, and then shining its light to the observer. He posits that it really hasn't happened until the observer does his observing. Even if the light would have had to happen billions of years ago in order for the observer to see it today.

Robert says, "According to quantum physics the past is indefinite and exists only as a spectrum of possibilities." This is true for the very small scale. The microscopic. A unified theory has not unified it with the macrocosm or reality as we know it. The author posits a biocentric universe in which the mind influences the matter or at least very small waves and particles.

He differentiates between the brain and the mind saying that the brain is post-temporal local, and the mind is pre-temporal local. Which is to say that the brain is made of matter, and the mind is not matter.

> *If the mind were so simple that we could understand it, then we would be so simple that we couldn't.*
>
> —GEORGE E. PUGH.

## Past Magic

I don't know whether we can change the past or not. There are some very smart people out there who think we could. And some who think we can't. Two viewpoints and one event. Hmmm. Didn't we just talk about that? If we were to change the past, how would we know that we had? It is changed. And it would no longer need changing. Because it was already done. Already done is something I can wrap my mind around. Already done is easy, and I like easy.

The past is already done. And so is the changed past already done. It happens in the realm of the unknown. Emerson describes it as "Here we stand before the secret of the world where being passes into appearance and unity into variety." I do know that when I step into what I call zero point, there is nothing there. And from that location, I can see infinite possibility. I would call that the realm of Magic. And there is no past or future, only the present moment.

# Co-Creation through Divine Perfection

*Wisdom Intent and Co-Creation*

Co-Creation is when we align our intention with the intention of the Universe, and together, we bring forth what we desire. The Universe desires to evolve and requires us to adapt to the infinite possibilities that it puts in front of us. The adaptation is successful or not. When it is successful then we evolve together into something new and hopefully wonderful. To the Universe all things are wonderful. To us, we aren't so sure. That is where Divine Perfection comes in.

*Divine Perfection*

Divine Perfection occurs when something turns out for the better when we originally thought it wasn't so good. Maybe a silver lining or maybe simply a different perception about what was good. Like the story about the Chinese man whose son brought home a horse. Maybe it's lucky and maybe it isn't. Divine perfection isn't about the perception of luck. It's about the Universe having a better idea about what needs to happen than we do. But we are a part of the Universe, so we get a vote. Wisdom is about allowing what has occurred and accepting that it might be for the best. We just don't know why yet. And we still get a vote. So, what do we vote for?

*Caucus Your Life*

I am reminded of the democratic caucuses that were run recently in Iowa and Nevada. People could vote early, and they had to put their first, second, and third picks on the ballot so that when the time came and the votes were cast, if their first candidate didn't make it into the top 15 percent, then their second or third choice would be given their vote. I wonder what would happen if we applied this process to our lives?

People generally care about three things: health, wealth, and relationships. After that they care about their spiritual connection to the Universe or God. What order they place them in is based on the conditions present in their lives. If they have a lot of illness or chronic pain, then health becomes the number one priority. If they are healthy, then relationship or wealth becomes number one. If they are in a good relationship, then wealth becomes the priority.

It's possible that people have need in all three areas. Then, they are usually struggling. They don't know which their priority is. Then, they are confused. But most people usually know which issue or issues they want to work on. We all have some work to do in all areas, although some rich people don't seem to think they need to work on the wealth area of their lives, until they do.

When one of these areas is good, then a fourth area is let into the mix, and that is often a person's spiritual relationship with the Universe. There is a small group of spiritually minded people who make their relationship to God or the Universe the most important thing in their lives.

So, where do we start? We pre-vote and write down our first second and third priorities. Then we show up at the caucus or at a class. (I list some classes on my website.) They take classes from an institution like a university or locally from the yoga center or online from someone like me. There are hundreds out there. So, I see some wisdom in caucusing your life.

## Super Tuesday and Your Life

What if you *Super Tuesdayed* your life? What if on one day you showed up for yourself in all areas in such a big way that you could declare yourself a winner in all areas of your life? How do you do that? First, you choose a day. It would help if it were a Tuesday. Then focus your intention on each of those areas of your life in the order that you need to. And by saying to yourself, *It's easy. In fact it's so easy that it is already done and the Universe has done it for me and all I have to do is join the Universe in seeing it through by living the experience that is showing up right here, right now. Woohoo! Let's celebrate!*

It might seem like you are accepting the status quo. But you are accepting a status quo that is already changing into something else. And something else and something else. You are accepting the change that you see occurring before your eyes. And you are helping it along by taking classes and reading books and also by reading your favorite blog! And as you share your changing self, the Universe is also changing. Together we are Co-Creating a new world with us in it. That is the wisdom of Intent and Co-Creation and Divine Perfection.

## Co-Creation through Purpose

*Awareness and Focus*

Awareness is when you pause and step back and see all that is surrounding you. It is an awareness of infinite possibilities and an awareness of your immediate surroundings. Focus is when you see only what is ahead of you and the path you are currently on. Focus directs your attention. It delineates your path. Where you put your *attention,* there goes your *intention.* And there goes the energy of what happens. Equal and opposite reaction.

You focus on what's wrong and you get more of what's wrong. You focus on what's right and you get more of what's right. Focus on what you want and not on what you don't want. That is the power of focus. Focus is a kind of intense energy. It's a lot like the focus of a camera. It narrows things down.

Awareness is fuzzy and widespread. It helps keep you safe by keeping you informed of your surroundings. Awareness also informs you of infinite possibilities. Awareness is being, while focus is more akin to doing. Awareness is in the present moment. So is focus, but there is a little more future to it because you are going somewhere.

*Both at the Same Time*

What if you could be aware and focused at the same time? You can. How? Come into the present moment. Look at something. Then allow your eyes to go soft and see all around you even in the back of your head. This is awareness. Now go back to focus. Keep your focus straight ahead. Go back and forth from focus to fuzzy awareness. Do this several times. Eventually you will realize that you are doing both at the same time. You are doing and being in the present moment.

Acting from this state is efficient, Joyful, and in alignment with the Universe. You are going with the flow of energy. You can choose from infinite possibilities and get something done at the same time.

## Do We Really Channel?

I was thinking this morning that there is no such thing as channeling. How can there be when we are really all one in unity consciousness? So then aren't we really listening to ourselves? I know people who channel or have channeled books. Is it that they are really listening to themselves? If we are all one, then God separates us so that he can know and experience himself. So, we separate or pretend to be individuals. Isn't it the same thing with guides and channeling? Some might say that the channel is an alter ego. We are really talking to ourselves or our higher selves.

Thought forms hang out in space. If we can believe that there is space and separation. We hear them and think that they are our thoughts. Or sometimes we think they are channeled thoughts and we give them a name. Abraham or Ellias or Mother Mary. When many people focus on the same entity, it or she can be very powerful. Also, the intensity of our focus fuels the power. So, does she or he exist? Yes. In the same way that we exist. We are both focused energy creations.

## Whose Thought Is This?

This morning I bilocated (actually, multi-located) to stand in front of a group, and I sprayed rose water into their open mouths. I wanted to share the energetic knowledge of the rose. I told them to listen to the rose. I told them that she had something to say to them. I saw the energy going into the pineal gland and the workings of the brain. I thought, *Well, it's working.* And then I thought that this was not my thought but the thought of someone else. Who was I hearing? My friend Leslie? This was the thought of one person in the group, and not my own. I don't usually see the workings of the brain.

We often hear another's thoughts, and think of them as our own. I certainly hear my husband's thoughts often. He will walk into the house and start to tell me about someone, and I will name who he is talking about before he does. Long-married couples often do that. We are very attuned to each other. Friends often finish the other's sentences.

All thought is out there, and we can hear those thoughts if we choose to listen. Sometimes we hear them even if we don't choose to, and we think that they are our own. One good way to practice listening is to talk to animals, trees, and rocks. They are a good source because they are honest and don't lie. Although checking on the veracity of the communication can be difficult.

You can have a friend ask you a question about their cat, then ask the cat and check on the answer with your friend. This will help with your veracity.

I had this experience with Asia Voight, an animal communicator. She asked a class to tell her if her cat had ever had kittens. I asked the cat, and I heard, *No, absolutely not.* So, I said, *No.* But what I saw in my mind was her cat wheeling kittens down the sidewalk pushing them in a stroller. My mind said, *No*, and my vision said, *Yes.* We need to practice communication to ascertain the right answer. The correct answer was *yes.* I got that answer, but I listened to my mind and words.

*Accuracy*

My vision is more accurate for me than words. In a vision, something just appears. I don't think it. My mind thinks and ascertains. It analyzes and comes up with an answer. But my visionary mind just pops up. As does my knowing. This is clairvoyance and clairsentience.

So, do we channel?

Yes and no. Not a very satisfying answer. Thought is out there as is the energy of another, which is not really another but ourselves creating a temporary separation to experience another. We do this for the experience of it, so that we can know the other and know ourselves even better. Yes and no.

## Co-Creation through Energy

So how does one bilocate? I was reading *Beyond Biocentrism* by Robert Lanza on Christmas Day, when it came to me that bilocation is like the double-slit electron experiment performed in 1909 by Sir Geoffrey Taylor. The experiment shows that whether an entity exists as either a wave or a particle depends on the observer. How does this apply to bilocation?

I observe myself in another place. Now, granted, that is a lot of energy. Much more than a tiny wave particle. But I see myself first as a light being. And second as a body of densified light. So, when I look at myself standing "over there," I have in that flash of a second, sent the wave particle of myself over there, and yet I am here at the same time doing the observing and it makes no difference whether I am bilocating or multi-locating. I am simply observing myself "there." That gives new meaning to the aphorism "seeing is believing." Or more correctly "believing is seeing." Wayne Dyer always said, "you'll see it when you believe it." And I do.

The same could be said about morphing into something. Like when I morphed into a horse on stage in Sedona in front of an audience. I wrote about that experience in *From Heartache to Joy*. It is also called shapeshifting. The event was filmed. Some people saw the horse. Some saw a very long face. And some will see it yet in the future. Hundreds of animals were thrown at me when I was on stage. I also did all of those and at the same time. How was that possible? I don't know how, but I know that it happened. I was the observer of myself. But so was the audience. This certainly calls into question the veracity of a witness at a crime scene. Is what they see even relevant?

We ourselves are light beings who already exist as all possibilities. "All possibilities simultaneously exist until a single one materializes upon observation" (Robert Lanza). I simply observe myself as the other or as several others.

*Beyond Biocentrism* goes on to say that locality is a kind of "superposition" in which all materiality is waiting to be materialized. Anything that could happen exists on some level, waiting to materialize. The act of observation causes the electron to leave probability and enter reality. I would call this the energy of Co-Creation from infinite possibility.

# Sacred Technologies of Co-Creation

*Techniques for Co-Creation through Intention*

1. **Grounding through Your Feet**. Feel into the earth with the energy of your feet. Tickle the center of the earth. Take a deep breath. Imagine that you have copper strands from the bottom of your feet going way down to the center of the earth. Watch and allow as the copper tendrils conduct the earth energy up into your feet, and then allow it to go up into your heart and out through your crown. Do this three times.

2. **Grounding through Your Knees**. For grounding into the earth with the energy of your knees, watch as you send silver strands of energy down into the earth from your knees. See yourself as a silver being standing on a silver energy field that is at the top of several hundred feet of silver soil. All is silver, and it spreads out horizontally across the earth. Stay in this place for several breaths.

3. **Clairsentience from the Heart.** For feeling, go into your heart. Expand out as big as the universe. Ask your heart what it knows about this. Ask all of your questions from this place. This is learning to know from the place of feeling awareness.

4. **Claircognizance from the Heart-Mind.** Join your heart with your mind. Bring your mind down into your heart. Or you can bring your heart up into your mind. Reside there. From this place ask a question and step into the answer. Feel into it with your heart-mind or allow it to pop up. Communicate from this place of knowing awareness.

5. **Morning Prayer**. Pick one word for the day and look for that aspect, condition, or tool throughout your day.

6. **Align.** Align yourself with that aspect. It will align you with your path. Check throughout your day. Are you still noticing that word?

7. **No Matter What.** Say three times, *I now choose to stay on my path, no matter what.*

*Techniques for Co-Creation through Joy*

8. **Grace toward Others.** *I* (state your name) *acknowledge that I will speak and act in grace with kindness to others in all that I say and do.*

9. **Grace toward Self.** *I* (state your name) *acknowledge that I will act in grace with kindness to myself.*

10. **Allow Others.** *I* (state your name) *acknowledge that I will listen to the ideas of others. I will allow them to have their own ideas.*

11. **Respect Self.** *I* (state your name) *acknowledge that I will respect myself in everything that I do and say.*

12. **Respect Others.** *I* (state your name) *acknowledge that I will respect others in all that they do and say.*

*Techniques for Co-Creation through Love*

13. **Yes to the Universe.** Say three times, *I* (state your name) *now accept that I Co-Create with the Universe. I say* Yes *to the universe.*

14. **Yes to Myself.** Say three times, *I* (state your name) *now say* Yes *to myself.*

*Techniques for Co-Creation through Divine Perfection*

15. **Noticing.** Increase your ability to notice. Notice what is in front of you. Then ask, *What else is there about this? What else might I notice?*

16. **Categories.** Make a list of the things you would like to change in your life. Determine which category or categories they fall into—life, health, love, spirituality, or Abundance. Do you have more than one category? Pick one to focus on.

17. **Ask for Help.** Ask the universe to bring into your life the right class, book, or person to help with that change. Notice when that help shows up. Take action. Your action is aligning yourself with the Universe.

*Technique for Co-Creation through Purpose*

18. **Focus and Awareness**. Come into the present moment. Look at something. Then allow your eyes to go soft and see all around you even in the back of your head. This is awareness. Now go back to focus. Keep your focus straight ahead. Go back and forth from focus to fuzzy awareness. Do this several times. Eventually you will realize that you are doing both at the same time.

*Technique for Co-Creation through Energy*

19. **Over There.** Pick any spot. See yourself as an energetic body "over there." An energy being. Full of light. Pull it back. Send it out and pull it back. Do this several times. When you are comfortable, have the energy being turn around and see an energy being where you are currently standing. And then pull the energy back to "over there." Now the awareness of your current location has become the "over there." See the "now here" from over there. Pull the energy back to where you are standing. In which location are you? Which have you chosen? Remember when you are done to always pull all your energy back to you. You don't want to leave it sprinkled around the universe. Do this only to the degree that you are comfortable. It should be fun.

# CHAPTER 10

# ABSOLUTE DIVINE PERFECTION

 It is meant to be, but you need to participate in it.

## Divine Perfection through Synchronicity

*Synchronicity: The Dishes*

Dishes are not my favorite things to do. But I accept that I need to do them. I do love a clean kitchen. And I like it a little better each time I pick something up and put it away or wash a few of the dishes or put a few in the dishwasher. Like most things in my life, I do them a little bit at a time. Rarely do I tackle the whole thing unless time constraints suggest I have to. This morning I put a few of the dishes away from the dishwasher, not all. I do a few as I get my morning coffee and am waiting for the Keurig to make the cup. After a few cups, the dishes are mostly done.

This morning when I came in from feeding the horses, my husband was finishing up the dishes. This is almost unheard of. He almost never does the dishes. So, I thanked him and went back to my morning blog. Acceptance, gratitude, celebration, and change. Try it. It works!

Was my husband's doing the dishes at the same time I was writing about acceptance, gratitude, and celebration a synchronous event? What made him do the dishes on this particular morning? The more we recognize synchronicity and divine perfection, the more it shows up. It's not mysterious, you say. He did the dishes, not the Universe. Yes, but after fifty-plus years of marriage, I think it's pretty synchronistic. I accept and I am grateful.

## Definitions

Carl Jung said that synchronicities are "acausal, meaningful coincidences" or "acausal parallelisms." The dictionary says that they are "simultaneous occurrences." Jung attached meaning to the occurrences. I call them Cosmic Coincidences, because I attach the relationship to the Universe. I believe the Universe is communicating with us through these coincidences. It is trying to get us to pay attention.

Divine Perfection is a little different. Divine Perfection is when something occurs and you think that it is negative, and then later on you discover that it is really a good thing. As we more and more accept the Divine Perfections that occur around us, we also see the cosmic coincidences that occur. The more we see the Cosmic Coincidences, the more we see the Divine Perfection in those occurrences.

Absolute Divine Perfection is seeing the perfection of the divine perfection. We look at something and say, *Wow, that was perfect*. And then we step back and say, *Wow, it was perfect that I saw it as perfect*. It seems as though we are talking double talk. But we aren't. We are simply stepping into the world of absolute divine perfections, and we call it what it is.

## Freedom and Synchronicity

This morning's meditation was Freedom. I asked to be shown what freedom feels like.

> *I see chaos and fire. And out of the struggle and burning of chaos, there grows an orange sunset. The color of freedom is sunset orange with soft peach and lavender. The movement of the energy was not peaceful and blue but moving and intense. I thought about the freedom of democracy and how we take it for granted. Our forefathers knew that if we were too complacent, we would lose the freedoms that we have. I thought of the immigrants coming to this nation seeking to*

*be free of the oppressions they are suffering. This nation has been a haven for freedom seekers.*

So, the energy of freedom is the energy of a sunset. It is moving, intense, ending, and beautifully calming all at the same time.

## *An Opportunity*

How do we change the relationship we have with our conditions? First, we accept and acknowledge them. Then we act in gratitude for them. Then we celebrate those conditions. By the time we celebrate them we discover that the conditions have changed. We don't accept them because we want them to change. We accept them because we have found a way to be okay with them or with something good about them. Like the lesson we are learning or the opportunity they have given us. The opportunity might be *to be or act differently*.

# Divine Perfection through Joy

The more Joy we feel, the more Divine Perfection we experience in life. But do we notice it? We notice Divine Perfection when we choose to notice it. We are in a better state of mind for choosing when we are in Joy. Divine Perfection exists everywhere and at all times. The universe is never wrong about what it is doing. We might not agree with it. We might think that we know better how things should happen. But we don't.

When we are in Joy, it seems that things are going the way we want them to. So, it is easy to agree with what the Universe is doing. With how things are going. If we are sad, or in grief, then we don't agree, and we are often in opposition to what is happening. We are also in opposition if we are in struggle, hate, or anger.

Divine Perfection occurs not just when things are going our way. It is always about when things are going the Universe's way. They are going to go that way anyway. So why not agree that the way they are going is Divine Perfection? Remember, Divine Perfection means that things will ultimately turn out for the better. We don't know how yet or why. But they will turn out for the better.

So, you ask, *But how can we be happy about the wars and deaths?* We aren't happy about those things. But we are happy that we are alive and that we live to experience another day. And we are happy that those around us are here to also experience another day. It is the experience that we are happy about. And we might as well be Joyful about it. It feels better than the alternative.

# Divine Perfection through Love

## *Allow Love*

Divine perfection is experienced when we allow love. It is experienced through the *unconditionality* of love. Through the acceptance, gratitude, and celebration of the experiences of life. When we celebrate our life, more of what we just celebrated occurs. Why does that happen? Because we have noticed the Divine Perfection that exists. But what about when something bad happens. How do we celebrate that?

## *Luck: Maybe*

Luck is a funny thing. We think that something is not good or unlucky, and also that something is good and lucky, and it turns out to be the opposite. I usually think of this in the negative, and it turns out for the better. Rarely do I think of it in the positive sense, and it turns out for the worse. But it can. Especially if we are so driven that something has to be a certain way, and life would be wonderful if it were just that way. But what if something even more wonderful were out there? Why should we limit ourselves to only one thing, our idea of wonderful? What if the Universe had planned something even more spectacular? Shouldn't we let that in?

Every morning before I get out of bed I say, *I wonder what wondrous, magical thing will happen today.* I say that three times. And then I begin my day. Saying this is a combination of gratitude and wonder for the day and for the wonderful things that I know are about to occur. Then it is my job to get out of bed and enjoy my day.

### The Dance of Divine Perfection

It was during Conscious Breathing with Zach Rehder in Kona, Hawaii, in 2015 that I encountered the dance of Divine Perfection for the first time. Zach asked us to share one word or term that described our experience. My term was *Divine Perfection*. Divine Perfection had come up to me and introduced herself. She asked, *Would you dance with me?* and I said *yes*. I learned from that experience that *not only Divine Perfection but life and all energy is a dance,*

Sometimes we have an experience and it is not what we would have chosen to do or be, but it was. It happened. Sometimes we are aware that everything happens in Divine Perfection. When we have that awareness, we might realize that things have turned out better than we could have ever hoped for. God has a better plan for us than we do. If we know that, we are less frustrated when things happen. We need to quit trying to think that we are better than God, and just allow. We can't change it anyway. It is Divine Perfection. And it is a dance. Enjoy the dance.

When we step into unconditional Love, the Universe greets us with spectacular occurrences that we call Cosmic Coincidences, and we begin to notice Divine Perfection. Everything is already perfect. We aren't lucky or unlucky.

 We can't do more nor can we create faster than God.

## Divine Perfection through Abundance

How perfect is Abundance as a platform? Of course, it's perfect. If you don't like this resolution you can try another and another. Abundance creates forward movement infinitely. You might think everything will stagnate because it's already perfect. That it won't move. But that's not true. It is always in motion. Energy has to move. The thing that keeps it moving is always another choice. Another possibility.

Divine perfection of what exists is not stagnant. The Universe is always asking, *And how about over here? And over here?* It is the infinite abundance of the Universe that allows the Divine Perfection of what it is to be in a constant state of becoming the next perfect thing.

## Divine Perfection through Peace

*Synchronicity and Peace*

Synchronicity happens all the time. But we tend to notice it around us when we are in a state of Peace or when we are acting in Grace. We notice it then because we are moving slowly enough, or we have stopped moving. Peace is quiet. Peace is not moving. Grace is quietly moving and moving with flow.

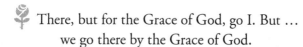 There, but for the Grace of God, go I. But …
we go there by the Grace of God.

*Grace*

A web search of *grace* says, "Grace means all the good gifts we enjoy freely in life." A thesaurus says, "elegance, refinement, beauty, style, poise, and kindness."

Grace is Peace in movement. It is the smooth flowing motion of all things that are in alignment with the universe. When we are moving quietly, we are able to notice the Divine Perfection that surrounds us.

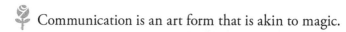 Communication is an art form that is akin to magic.

## Divine Perfection through Magic

*The Magic of Communication*

I looked back at what I wrote in the chapter on communication in *From Heartache to Joy*. I drew the card for Communication this morning in my

Morning Prayer. The animal that anchors that chapter is the *ant*. Ant is in constant communication with his fellow community.

The word *communication* suggest that it is about community. Our senses inform how we take information in and how other people receive information from us. We also communicate with the earth and all that is around us, and we communicate with Source or God, and our guides.

## Hearsay

We communicate with the earth when we ground ourselves. And we communicate with the earth when we talk to a tree or a rock. The tree and rock are already attached energetically, or one might say unified with the earth. We are also unified with the earth, but we pretend that we are separate. Talking with trees and rocks is like talking to the earth. Trees are already in direct communication with the earth. So, talking with them is like hearsay. But it's honest hearsay. Secondhand knowledge. In the same way that talking to any guru or teacher is secondhand knowledge.

## Direct Communication

Talking with animals is a little more complicated. Our minds get in the way of direct communication. We tend to interpret what we hear or know from that communication, and our interpretation can misinform us.

Communicating with other people is a lot like communicating with animals. Except that we have language, which in itself is imprecise. And the more precise we try to make it, the further away from the truth we go. Language limits us. It traps us into believing that the limitations it poses are real. Then of course we add our own interpretation based on our perceptions, which are based on our history. This is at least four or five degrees of separation away from the truth. It's like the game of telephone and sending the word *red* around a circle and having it come out *purple* at the end.

*Synchronicities*

The Universe is always communicating with us. It sends us messages in the form of synchronicities. It tells us that everything is okay and is really in Divine Perfection. It asks us, *Have you looked at this, and how about this over here?* The Universe is in constant communication with us to put us on the right path. It will put a billboard in front of us or the right book or a phone call. The Universe is always trying to help us. We simply have to be aware and notice it when it does.

Our words have the power of Magic. We should utter them with care. And we should also accept that no matter what we say, our words are already in Divine Perfection.

# Divine Perfection through Intention

*The Cosmic Coffee Connection*

I was staying at the Mauna Lani hotel in Hawaii with my friend Leslie. We were attending a multidimensional being retreat. I got up at 5 a.m. to do my Morning Prayer before the sessions began. Leslie was still asleep.

I made coffee to take with me to the beach. The coffee overflowed and spilled down the front of the cupboard. There were coffee grounds everywhere. I cleaned up the mess, got my coffee, and proceeded to go outside to embrace the sunrise.

John called from Wisconsin. He was drinking his morning coffee. He was upset because his coffee had overflowed and spilled down the front of the cabinet. He said that there were coffee grounds everywhere. I told him what had happened to me. He was in Wisconsin. I was in Hawaii.

He said, "Talk about cosmic coincidence and connection."

I just laughed.

*Synchronicities, and Intention*

The more we notice and recognize the Divine Perfection or synchronicities around us, the more they occur. Sometimes they are small occurrences like a log rolling off the fire in the fireplace, and that disturbance calling my attention to something else that is going on. I have to get up from my writing and fix the log. But then my thought changes, and something magical occurs. I notice or think about something that I need to write. Or a pen rolls on the floor, and I bend over to pick it up only to discover the keys I had misplaced.

These are tiny incidences that occur every day. When we link them to Divine Perfection or a synchronicity, then they become more powerful and they occur more often. Sometimes the coincidences are bigger, and we can't help but notice them. Like the story about the coffee grounds.

When our *attention* gets called to something, then we have the ability to *intend* something. Attention and focus are interlinked. So, intending to have more incidences of synchronicities and recognizing the Divine Perfection of it all cause more of both to occur. We accept the Divine Perfection and we recognize the synchronicities. Intention increases frequency and power.

*We are the offspring of the force evolving into new universes.*

—Stephen Hawley Martin

## Divine Perfection through Purpose

*The Step from Okay to Purpose*

What traits do we need to develop if we want to stay on the path and prosper? Stephen Hawley Martin asks this question in his book, *The Force Can Be with You.* "You can Love" is one of those traits. The lower forms of life like earthworms don't care for their young. Frogs don't. Primates and humans do. Love is essential to the survival of our species. Love includes cooperation and harmony. There is an evolutionary push toward harmony.

What does this mean for the survival of our species with the divisiveness that we see everywhere? Well, maybe not everywhere, but certainly in our own politics and in the Middle East, Africa, and Central America. I choose not to look at that divisive behavior for too long. *The Force* is attracted to whatever we are looking at and where we put our attention. I acknowledge the divisiveness and I move on. What do I move on to?

## Okay

This morning I started with okay. Or *Okay. Smart Lookup* gives us definitions for *okay* of "right, satisfactory, fine"; and as a noun, "approval." It is also a verb: "to give approval to." With these definitions, I feel that somehow the judgement is coming from outside myself to make it right, when the only judgement that exists is currently inside me, making it right or wrong. And it is never wrong. It is always in Divine Perfection. The Universe or Force cannot act in any other way. So, we start with letting go of judgement and allowing what is. That is one definition for aligning with *okay*. Beyond okay is what we step into.

## Purpose

What do we step into? We step into our purpose. Hindus call it *dharma*. The eternal and inherent nature of reality. I would say that our purpose is our soul's purpose. It is like the world is a huge puzzle and we only fit when we are our own unique piece. If you consider life a gift, then you could consider dharma a gift. But it is more of a skill that we practice, when we align with our purpose.

Ask yourself, *If money were not an issue, what would I want to do in life?* The answer you give is what is closest to your purpose.

The infinite mind and "the force be with you" mean the same thing. It is the job of your brain to integrate your personal portion of consciousness with your body. Research shows that consciousness can exist independent of the brain, however.

Force continues to push its creation to evolve. Intelligence came first. The species that are too far down a particular path fail to adapt and they die. Adaptability is another trait our species needs, and any species needs to survive.

## A Becoming Universe

If a universe is becoming and every drop of water is leaving something behind, then what is the universe becoming? It is becoming what we choose individually and cooperatively to become as those individual drops of water. We take the ocean with us. We are the ocean. Drops and the whole at the same time. Our drop is a hologram of the whole ocean. By definition, a hologram contains the entirety of the whole. We are not less than or more than. We are.

From *okay*, I accept the Divine Perfection that is, and I step into the world that I discover is already aligned with my purpose. *Whaaaat?* you say. *It's already done?* Yes, it's already done in the Divine Perfection that it is. And I can just stroll along. How easy. And fun and Joyful. Yes, it is.

## Divine Perfection through Energy

What is the energy of Synchronicity and Divine Perfection? It's the energy of *Oh, that's strange. I wonder why that just happened.* It's the energy of the cosmic coincidence that happens when someone you haven't thought about in a long time suddenly calls you on the phone and you say *I was just thinking about you.* What does that feel like?

*Cosmic Coincidence Energy*

Cosmic Coincidence is energy like the one last night when my husband and I were going into the movie theater and he stopped and said, *How about we use that coupon you have for Texas Road House after the movie?* I had just thought about doing that not ten seconds before. I told him I was just thinking about that. Neither of us had thought about that in months and in fact the coupon when I checked it was more than a year old and out of date. That's a cosmic connection between two people. That connection occurs when we listen deeply to our own thoughts or we are quiet.

*Divine Perfection Energy*

What is the energy of Divine Perfection? It is the energy that occurs when we think that something is bad or wrong, but it turns out to be good. When we say, *Oh no, this happened*, and then we say, *Oh yay, this happened.* The happening is really in the Divine Perfection path of the Universe. It happened for a reason that the Universe knows. We don't know and ours is not to ask *why* but to say *okay*. And then to say, *How can I help make this better?* I accept that it is. And then ask the question.

The energy of Divine Perfection is the energy of acceptance. And then the energy of realizing that it really occurred, offering a better result. It is a little like the energy of a silver lining. But it isn't the same. It is one thing and then it is really another. We need to let go of the energy of all judgement. Then we can be in the energy of the freedom that occurs when we let go of judgement. We are free to feel that everything is in Divine Perfection. When we recognize the energy, we get even more of it. More cosmic coincidences and more Divine Perfection.

# Sacred Technologies of Absolute Divine Perfection

*Techniques for Divine Perfection through Love:*

1.  **Past Incidences.** Make a list of the incidences that occurred in the past that you might have thought were bad but then turned out to be for the better.
2.  **Today's Incidences.** List the incidents of divine perfection that occurred that day. Try to notice ten. Do this for one week.
3.  **Morning Prayer.** Ask God to show you what Divine Perfection looks like.
4.  **Early Morning.** When you get up in the morning, say, *I wonder what wondrous, magical thing will happen **today**.* Then Notice it. Then watch it happen. Give gratitude when it does. The more you do this, the more you notice the magical things that are already happening around you.
5.  **Throughout the Day.** Repeat as often as you can remember to throughout the day, *I wonder what wondrous, magical thing will happen **next**?* Then watch it happen. Give gratitude when it does.

*Techniques for Divine Perfection through Peace*

6. **I am love. You are love.** Say, *I am love. I am light. I am infinite.* Say, *You are love. You are light. You are infinite.* Say each three times. Notice the difference. Where does each phrase reside in you? Bring the two locations together into one source point and say the phrases again.

7. **Moving Meditation.** Use the above phrase as a walking meditation. Say, *I am love. I am light. I am infinite.* Say, *You are love. You are light. You are infinite.* I use it on each step I take or each stroke I swim. What this exercise does is it allows you to embody the statement. It embodies *I am love.*

8. **Create an Alignment Button.** Notice which direction your spirit is going in. Create an alignment button on your spiritual computer. Then hit your alignment button. When you align with your spirit, you act in Peace.

9. **Say the Morning Prayer** and ask to be shown what Peace feels like. Ask God to show you the Peace that surrounds you in life. Notice where it appears in the rest of your day.

10. **Reflect** in your journal on the following questions:
    - What did you see or feel during your Morning Prayer?
    - Where did you experience Peace today?
    - Where did you align with spirit today?
    - Did you see Peace where you had never seen it before?
    - What color was it?
    - What did it smell like?
    - Does Peace have a taste?
    - Where is Peace located in my body?

*Techniques for Divine Perfection through Intention*

11. **Not Bad but Good.** Make a list of past incidents that you thought were bad but then turned out to be for the best.

12. **Incidents of Divine Perfection.** List the incidents of Divine Perfection that occurred today or this week or month or year

when something happened that you thought was bad and turned out to be for the best. Try to notice ten.

13. **Cosmic Coincidences.** List the incidents of cosmic coincidences that occurred today. Try to notice ten. Do this for one week.

14. **Morning Prayer.** Ask God to show you what Divine Perfection looks like.

## *Journaling*

15. Reflect in your journal on the following questions:
    - What did I see or feel during my Morning Prayer?
    - Where did I experience Divine Perfection today?
    - Where did I align with Divine Perfection today?
    - Did I see Divine Perfection where I had never seen it before?
    - What color was it?
    - What did it smell like?
    - Does Divine Perfection have a taste?
    - Where is Divine Perfection located in my body?

## *Technique for Divine Perfection through Purpose*

16. **Already Whole.** Say three times, *I am already whole and complete.*

17. **No Fixing.** Say three times, *There is no need for fixing and changing.*

18. **Acceptance.** Say three times, *I accept what is. It is okay. It is better than okay.*

19. **My Purpose.** Say three times, *As I step into a new world, I step into my purpose.*

20. **New World.** Say three times, *The new world is my purpose.*

## *Techniques for Divine Perfection through Energy*

21. **Synchronicity Energy.** Ask, *What does synchronicity feel like?* Then feel it.

22. **Divine Perfection Energy.** Ask, *What does Divine Perfection feel like?* Then feel it.

# CHAPTER 11

# ABSOLUTE PURPOSE

🌹 The purpose of life is to live a life of purpose.

—Fortune cookie

## Purpose of Purpose

I recently had a fortune cookie that said, *The purpose of life is to live a life of purpose.* But what is a life of purpose and what is the purpose of living a life of purpose?

*Dream: Entrainment*

> *I am lying on the ground with my face flat against it. Then I notice that I am flowing forward. It is as if I have become a puddle. I like flowing. It is such an easy way to move forward. Then I wonder if I could flow upward. I flow upward as if I am flowing up a wall. It is quite magical. I think, "This is fun." Then I think to just hang out up in the air. So, I rise up into the sky and look down. I think, "This is an easy way to get around. Just flowing."*

The next morning, I told John about my dream. He said, *Hmmm.* He told me that before he went to sleep, he was reading a book about writing.

It was a section on writing about objects. The objects he read about were puddles. Most examples were people jumping and splashing in puddles. But the last example was a person who became the puddle.

I said. *Hmmm. Synchronicity.*

He said *No, entrainment.*

I said. *Both.*

## Synchronicity and Entrainment

I often hear John's thoughts. Sometimes I hear him singing a song. I think that it might be my song. But I ask him what song is going through his head. I start singing a song and it is the exact same song that it is going on in his head. I know that it is not my song because I don't have songs going through my head. He does, twenty-four seven. Often I have a thought. We have a thought. I ask, *Was that my thought or yours?* Oftentimes we can't tell. That is entrainment. I guess we are like old clocks that are just tick tocking together.

Two are more powerful than one. The Universe brings us together in entrainment so that we are more powerful. So that we can live our purpose together more powerfully.

## Purpose Divine Perfection and Cosmic Coincidence

When I think of God, I can imagine a divine purpose. I would call that Divine Perfection. And that means that the right best thing always happens in the eyes of God. But when I think of the Force or the Universe, I cannot think of Purpose so easily. I can imagine that there is reaction and what I would call opportunity. I think the Universe is always suggesting and showing us a path. It encourages us to find and stay on our path. But I think that it is reacting to our own intent. I think that energy is reacting to energy. I don't think of it as a divine purpose. When I think of the Force, I think that energy and the reaction to energy are even more apparent. So my perception changes toward Purpose, depending on whether I refer to God, Source, Universe, or Force.

## *Who Is Telling?*

Purpose seems to infer that someone or something else is telling us what to do or why we are here. Or perhaps our purpose is only us telling ourselves why we are here. If we listened to our higher self, we would know why we are here. I believe that I am here to share my experience and Joy with the world. Or maybe only to share with anybody who cares to listen.

I believe we should follow no one and that we should find our own way. And I also believe that the Force puts people and situations in our paths so that we can stumble back on to our paths when we misstep. I believe that the energy of our misstep is reacted to by the Force. And that reaction is to put something in our way. We have to deal with that something to get back on our path.

When that something is a whisper, then it's relatively easy. When it's getting hit in the head by a two by four, then we have a major issue to deal with. A whisper is like standing in line at the grocery store. A two by four is a major illness. Both of these are reactions to our misstep. Experiencing a misstep does not mean that we are wrong. It means that we need to acknowledge something and move on with our purpose.

## *Aligning with Purpose*

What is your purpose? What makes your heart sing? What can you do for hours without stopping? What are you doing when you look up and time has flown by? What gives you the biggest grin?

Aligning ourselves with our purpose not only give us pleasure. It also makes the stumbling blocks on our path roll away. The path seems to magically clear. And we have an easier journey.

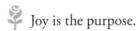 Joy is the purpose.

# Purpose through Joy

*Magnificence*

Magnificence is to Beauty as Glory is to Joy. Glory is a kind of celebration of Joy. And at first, I thought Magnificence is a kind of celebration of beauty. But *celebration* is not quite the right word. Maybe *beauty on steroids*. But that feels too negative. Magnificence is an increasing in intensity. An increasing in the complexity in design, such as when fractals are repeated in the design of a flower. Or of broccoli. Each group of florets is repeated in the next one smaller down. That is a fractal. And that is what I mean by increasing complexity in design. We call that beautiful and sometimes we call that magnificent.

But we also call the simple things magnificent. Like a lion's ruff or the colors of a sunset.

*Purity of Beauty*

So, what is Magnificence if it's not extreme simplicity or extreme repetitive complexity? It is so pure in what it is that its own perfect self seems to explode out from its center to the world, in the same way that beauty is an expression of the person, and that person shines that expression out. Magnificence is the expression of the purity of the person or object. And that purity is expressed outward to the world. It is a purity of simplicity or purity of complexity or repetition of form. Or purity of the in-between, as in a sunset. A purity of normalcy.

As people seek to look at the magnificent sunset or mountain or lion, many of us see the magnificence in a ladybug or a flower. Some of us who cook or garden see the magnificence of cauliflower or broccoli.

Beauty is also in the eye of the beholder. It is about our ability to see everything as beautiful. What we are is what we see. This would hold true for Magnificence also.

*Simplicity is the ultimate sophistication.*

—Leonardo da Vinci

## The Waterfall

I remember sitting in front of a waterfall in Pohnpei, a high part of the island of the Federated States of Micronesia. I was working there as chief architect. It was a Saturday. And I hiked to this waterfall to sit and maybe bathe in the glory of it. I was accompanied by a local gentleman who showed me the way.

As we sat and looked at the waterfall, he asked me, *Do you think that the waterfall is beautiful?*

I was surprised by the question. *Yes,* I said. *Don't you?*

*No,* he said. *It is just water. Not beautiful.*

I didn't ask him what he thought was beautiful. I should have. But I was young back then, and didn't know enough to be interested in such things. He didn't see the beauty. To me it was magnificent. Was it because of the rarity? Was it because I didn't have one in my backyard back home in Wisconsin?

## Perspective and Belief

I now know that the Marshallese (from the Marshall Islands, a low volcanic island in the central Pacific Ocean) don't see the color red. They don't distinguish it from brown. The color is the same to them. They call it *bururer.* Our own perspective, beliefs, and experiences in the world color our view of red. To me the waterfall was magnificent. To others it was just water. To me the sunset is magnificent. To others, the sun is simply going down before it gets dark.

I choose to see a magnificent world. I choose to see all things in it as magnificent. Why? Because looking at a flower and feeling the gasp on the inbreath and then having my breath stop is a magnificent feeling. It is beyond beauty. The feeling is magnificent. And isn't it better to feel magnificent than to think, *Just okay.* It's like the television ad that asks the question, *Do we want our surgeon to be just okay?* That's just water.

When we see magnificence around us, we ourselves become magnificent. We reflect what we see. We become the purity of ourselves. And isn't that our journey? To experience the magnificence that we already are? To experience the purity of ourselves?

I went out to feed the horses this morning. Before I edited this chapter. When I went out the sun was shining. That in itself was magnificent. We hadn't seen the sun for many days. I looked at the horses. I always see them as beautiful. But this morning, they were magnificent. The snow was magnificent. Everything was magnificent.

*Let life live through you.*

—RUMI

# Purpose through Love

## Truth, Presence, and Wonder

Truth is hiding under a rock, and Presence is right here lying in wait as Wonder hovers in anticipation of the next right action. I see this as I see that Truth is represented by Snake winding and unwinding. Presence is represented by Alligator lying in wait, and Hummingbird hovers in the anticipation of Wonder. There is no *the* in front of these animals. *The* represents an individual. And these animals represent the spirit of that animal in the shamanic sense. Truth, presence, and wonder are aspects of Love.

## Potentiality

Why is Truth hidden under a rock? Why don't we see it immediately? Why do we have to look for it? Truth is what is there even when we don't look at it. But what is there without us looking at it? The biocentrists tell us that nothing is there before we look at it. They tell us that we create what is there by our looking at it. But then what are we looking at if nothing is there?

The materialist says that only that which can be proven exists. Even though they agree that the person who is doing the observing is affecting the outcome of the observation. And some spiritualists would say that space is there with potentiality. I like potentiality. That gives me a clean slate to choose the life I want to live and to surround myself with the conditions that would make it easy to bring my choices into being. So, for me, the Truth is that potentiality exists.

## Causation

The Truth is also that the present moment is all that is. There is no past to inform or limit our current decisions. We can pretend and use the past to inform us so that we don't make the same mistakes. That is a good thing. But there is also the danger that the past will limit us in the present moment. If we believe in causation, then just like this statement, our present moment is dictated by the past. It is a limitation and we are locked into it. If we believe in causation, then our future is predicated on our present moment. But in the present moment, there is no past or future and there is no causation. There is only now and potentiality. When causation ceases to exist, we are free to choose whatever we decide. Funny to use a statement of causation to disprove causation!

The truth seems hidden under a rock, but it is in plain sight. The presence is always at our feet. Wonder hovers above the ground. It leans back slightly, takes a look, and then darts in.

Hover, back, dart in, repeat, hover, back, dart in, repeat. This is how Hummingbird acts. Wonder is a spiritual experience.

Truth and Presence are grounding unless we raise them up into the heart space where we consider our spirituality to reside. Then they seem spiritual. In truth there is no difference between what is grounded and what is spiritual. They are the same. We separate them so that we can take a look at the purity of their energies.

Together they all make up the totality or unity of God. They are just conditions and tools that we use to navigate this earth plane, living better and more easily. The science of materiality has sent people to the moon and has cures for diseases. Believing in that kind of materiality is useful to our lives. But there is another side to that coin. And that other side is not believing in our self-worth or our ability to choose what happens or the direction we take in our lives.

*The Experience*

If everything sat in the unity of all things or potentiality, we would feel and experience nothing. And we are here to experience. We are separate beings in order to have the experiences we are having. So, there is Truth, Wonder, and Presence with a past and a future. It exists so that we can explore why and wonder about it. So that we can ask, *What is the cause of this or that?* None of it is true beyond our wondering. It is simply a possibility of the Truth.

How does this help us in our lives? It gives us the power of choice. It allows us to unshackle ourselves from our beliefs and our past. It allows us to let go of any anxiety we hold about our future. It helps us to align three aspects of Love with the Universe. Those aspects are Truth, Presence, and Wonder.

 Free enough to know the value within you.

## Purpose through Abundance

*Magnitude*

The card I picked this morning was the Morning Prayer Card, the prayer itself. So, I picked another one. It was Magnitude. The picture on it was elephant and it said this: *Elephant sways in a dance of magnitude.* Ganesha removes the stumbling blocks in our paths.

Our path is what we follow in coming home to ourselves. One might ask, why do we have to follow anything if we are coming home to ourselves? Aren't we already here? The answer is *yes*. We are having an experience. We sometimes call that a journey. It only seems that we are going somewhere. Maybe because we are always moving. So, we think we must be going somewhere. That's what we tell ourselves. We could simply run in place. I think that's what we call *being*.

So, *Magnitude*. Elephant kicks the obstacles out of the way on a journey that doesn't really go anywhere so that we can take a path to the place where we are already standing. Good Grief! That's exhausting to think about and to do.

*Quality Dance*

Life is reflected to us in a dance of Magnitude. Magnitude is beyond size. It is a quality and not a quantity. It is not how big the elephant is, but how he moves in the dance. The dance goes from a tiny dot to infinity and back without any recognition of time or space. Perhaps there is an acknowledgement. But there is no stepping into. Just a dance back and forth. Magnitude does not become matter in time or space. We dance back and forth with all the polarities in our lives. Male and female, good and bad, right and wrong. Judgements always have two sides. This is the Dance of yin and yang.

It is the quality of Magnitude that we can perceive in this dance and not the materiality of size. In our hearts we perceive that quality. In our minds we perceive the quantity. Like a large piece of chocolate cake.

 That's where you need to go, and you need to go there.

# Purpose through Peace

*Peace in the Power of Grace and Bliss*

There is Peace in Grace and Bliss. There is also Peace in Power. And a great deal of Power in Peace. I can conceive of the Grace of Power but not the sweetness of power. Sweetness of power smacks too much of power over. What are the Power of sweetness and the Power of Bliss? Sweetness and kindness are a part of Christianity and Zen Buddhism. Both say that we should be sweet and kind. Kind to our neighbors. Jesus said that we should love our neighbors as ourselves. But I don't think he counted on us not loving ourselves very much.

*Grace*

We can't love another if we don't love ourselves. The love isn't in us to share. The same goes for kindness and sweetness. In my first book, *From Heartache to Joy*, I describe a meditation I had in which I saw a bear carrying a honey pot, and telling me to spread that honey to the world. I was dumbfounded because I didn't think that I had a sweet bone in my body. I considered sweet to be saccharine. And clingy and cloying. But that's not what sweetness is. It's kind and considerate. And just like love, you can't be kind and considerate with another until you are kind and considerate with yourself. How is it that we are kind to ourselves?

For me it's about not pushing myself too hard. About not trying to do too much. Why shouldn't I take a day off? Or allow myself to read a book or to take a nap? Or maybe taking a day and going for a drive and bumming? We used to do that a lot more. Or maybe getting more sleep? Lately I've been binge-watching too much television on Netflix. That's easy to do. And staying up too late and not getting enough sleep. Then I got a virus that knocked me out for two and a half days.

I wasn't being kind to myself. My body needed more sleep. That's the power of kindness.

## *Bliss*

What is the Power of Bliss? I think of Bliss as a very refined high energy that shines out from a person who is aware. Sometimes we call that person *enlightened*. We call them enlightened for a reason—because their light shines out from their being and it is visible to those who see him or her. Sometimes there is a corona from the head or sometimes the light shines out everywhere. Sometimes, it is momentary like a flash of light and sometimes it is continual. Or it can even be a glow all over the skin.

We talk about the light that shone forth from the great spiritual leaders, like Jesus or Buddha. Or even Gandhi. But I've also seen the glow from ordinary people. I once saw a young Christian girl in college who glowed all over. People were attracted to her for her Joy. And seemingly for no reason. People just couldn't get enough of her. I remember trying to figure out at the time why this was happening. She wasn't physically beautiful. She didn't have any obvious gifts or talents. So why did she attract so much attention? It was like watching moths fly into a light.

What is the power of Bliss? The power of Bliss is that it brings consciousness and awareness to all who come in contact with it, whether they are aware of it or not. It brings the light into the dark. That's a funny phrase bringing awareness to the unaware. Those who are unaware are brought into awareness, and yet they are unaware that it happened. Or maybe they do become aware of it.

## Rebirth

The metaphor of moths to a light holds true. I'm a little dismayed by the moths dying when they hit the flame, until I realize that with consciousness there is always a death and a rebirth. We have to die to our old ways in order to be reborn into the new world we wish to live in. One that we have chosen. Bliss offers the power of rebirth.

But how do you choose Bliss? Once you have felt it, you can call it up. You can recall the energy and you can return to it. It will be different because you are different. But that is okay.

If you have never felt it, I would start with awareness. Practice standing in awareness. Eventually you will find a very refined energy that I would call Bliss.

# Purpose through Magic

I recently did a "Lucia Light Session" with Katrina Chaudoir. Her literature says that the session "provides a deep limbic and central nervous system relaxation while gently stimulating the pineal gland/3rd eye and opening a space for visual exploration." She used the Lucia N°03 light system. When I first wrote this section, I put it in magic rather than energy. It could also easily go in the category of energy. But I also consider the technology quite magical.

## Weaver of Worlds

Katrina Chaudoir took notes as I did my session with the flashing Lucia N°03 light. The actual session is preceded by three demos in which various light frequencies are offered. Then the client selects the appropriate light frequency for the session.

These are Katrina's notes:

"1ˢᵗ Demo: Beautiful bold reds dancing into your session with joyful pinks and whites. Your energy is very whimsical yet protected and grounded. A very beautiful balance. Your many spirit guides came in right away.

"2ⁿᵈ Demo: Lots of whites came rushing in, flooding your being with cleansing energy. I'm hearing you are letting go of a lot of stagnant energy and blockages of things that no longer serve you. With joy, we are releasing them, thanking them for serving you up until this point and calling in an energy that will better serve your path here and now. More joy.

"3ʳᵈ Demo: There is a strong feline, large cat energy coming in for you today. And as I typed these words, a cheetah came in and sat next to your right side. A very strong protective force and very wise. Cheetah is saying, *There are a great amount of things in motion for you right now. Things are happening and are going to happen very fast.* To maintain focus and clarity on your path, call on Cheetah energy to help you stay on target. The amount of light you hold in your system is profoundly bright. You are such a Lightworker, and have been for many lifetimes."

## Her Reading of This Session

"My hands were set ablaze as your session began. The heat transferred from my palms to my fingertips, telling of the many lifetimes you have indeed worked with transforming energy into the magic of joy and love to help people find themselves once again and remember who they truly are. In this vision that came through for you today, you were a healer in your tribe and could morph into the energy of the Cheetah. Your wise, all-knowing eyes were comforting to your tribe members as they sought your guidance and counsel. You specialized in the field of empathy and helped beings who were grieving find the gifts. You helped ones with grief connect to their loved ones and helped them thin the veil to spirit, reminding them that there is no separation. You also helped beings who were ready to cross over and transition from their earthly vessels back to spirit. Also helping beings to come from spirit and enter their vessels.

"You have done a lot of work around being born, rebirthed, and dying. You were always finding compassion, understanding, and the deeper meaning behind even the hardest of situations Through your work, you innately taught others how one may access spirit on their own.

"You were known to be fearless in the art of tough love. You were one to give it to someone straight, and never sugarcoat anything. Though you spoke the truth, you did it in a diplomatic way that took out the punch, so to speak. You formed strong relationships of brotherhood and sisterhood in your work, and created a close inner weaving between all your tribe members. You were said by the leaders of your tribe to be the glue that brought everyone together. You were known by your people as 'The Weaver of Worlds.'

"There were many points when your light was shining so brightly that I had to put on my shades to see. Something that doesn't always happen."

*My Light Session Experience:*

My own experience of this light session was as follows:

> *Hard to believe it's only white light. The colors. I've never seen such colors. Different. Nice when the pulsating goes away, and it gets quiet. I can go into a big purple eye or soup. Sometimes, it would just go grey, then it would turn black and red and really powerful stuff. Then all combinations together.*
>
> *At one point, someone walks up. It is a big presence. Metatron.*
>
> *Then there is a shape, like the base of a stand, then it fades into nothing. It fades into grey or blue. At one point, it's a gorgeous lavender. The whole screen is lavender, then little dots of lavender. Then I am going down a tunnel.*
>
> *Mandalas are spinning and pulling me into a tunnel. Toward the end though, it goes into a big blue mushroom-like eye. There is a building and rectangular shapes. Mostly, there are lots of mandalas. Pulsing, fading, going in and out. I am reminded of a paper folding game moving my fingers. I open and close my imaginary paper structure over and over again. First in one direction and then in another. There is lots of that.*

*Body things. I stick my foot in and see what that looks like. Then I stick my right knee in. Then I decide not to control the journey. Then I let go of trying to do anything with anything.*

*I think about going through the wall and flying a little bit. There is lots of activity around that.*

*I see a Machine. The Machine is spinning. I can't help but see the machine spinning.*

*I am a Busy person. They call me dream weaver and energy weaver.*

It was after this experience that I began to call myself, *Weaver of Worlds.*

 The stage is more real than life itself.

## Purpose through Intention

*Question and Wonder*

This morning when I checked my blog posts, a reader had asked me how I write and get past what writers call writer's block. He was worried about the first fifteen minutes before his writing came through him.

In answering the question, I suggested he ask himself the question: *What gift can I give my readers today? What gift can I give myself today?* Hmmm. I give the gift of myself to myself and to my readers today! Thanks for that! I think I'll write about that gift. My reader's question has given me a gift.

*My Writing Practice:*

The following was my answer to him:

"I have a habit of doing what I call the Morning Prayer every morning. You can find that discussed in one of the blogs. Then I ask what should I be, see, or experience today? I wait and then the ideas come pouring in. I usually write about that. But I also write about whatever interesting experience I am having. I journal the experience with enough keywords to remember the event when I sit down to write.

"Also, I tend to leave a piece unfinished. There is always a sentence or two that needs finishing. When I start the next day, I finish the sentence and then it just keeps coming. So, leaving something undone is one way to get started again. It's like priming a water pump.

"Or I make notes about the next day. My journal is a good place for those notes. My own practice is to write first thing in the morning before I begin my day. I think that it's important to have a dedicated time. Having a dedicated time lets your body and mind know that it's happening now and you are ready."

*Wonder*

What I was going to write about this morning was Wonder. The card of Wonder was what I drew from my Morning Prayer Card deck. I have just begun using it myself these last few weeks. I created the deck for others. I thought that since things came to me so easily I didn't need my own cards. But I find that they are fun. I drew the Wonder card yesterday and seemed to ignore it. And I wrote about something else. But today I drew it again. So, I can't ignore it. But how does it fit in? How does Wonder fit into this conversation?

A couple of weeks ago, I offered my card deck to a friend and she picked out the hummingbird card of Wonder. She had been struggling with selling her company and with making all the decisions that the selling entailed. She was in a place where she had to halt and wait. And she was uncomfortable in that place of not doing. She saw when she looked at that card that she was exactly where she needed to be, *hovering in anticipation*.

It is a cosmic coincidence and it fits all at the same time. The picture on the card is of a hummingbird. Hovering. The line underneath says, *Hummingbird hovers in anticipation.*

Fast forward to today's question. The reader and writer are exactly where they need to be. Hovering in anticipation of what he will write. It is the moment when the wings move very fast and we are hovering.

Anticipation is very fast on the inside. And then zoom, we are flashing around writing or doing whatever it is that we do.

Wonder has the action of taking in a deep breath, almost a gasp, and then we lean forward and let out a sigh. The breath is very much a part of wonder. Even the hummingbird has this backward movement before he leans forward into his drink of nectar.

*Questions Are Gifts*

Maybe the gift of words is like the reward of nectar. That gift is my nectar and I share it with you. I didn't realize until today that questions themselves are gifts.

Why did I call this a cosmic coincidence or divine perfection? I called it that because two different events came together—the question on my blog site and the card of Wonder—to bring me to the idea that a question is a gift. When we ask God a question, we are giving him a gift. And he says, *Thank you and here is your gift.*

Our purpose is to align our Intention with the intention of the Universe. When we ask a question, we are directing our attention and the attention of the Universe toward a direction. The answer we get is a gift on that path.

## Purpose through Divine Perfection

Originally, I wrote this section about fires in Australia. But now I think it also applies to the fear and hatred that we see occurring with the Covid-19 virus, and the tragedy that is currently happening all over the world with the pandemic.

The acceptance of Divine Perfection in the face of tragedy is the ultimate in acceptance. It is our purpose to be stewards of the Earth. So, seeing the Divine Perfection in the fires in Australia is our purpose as stewards of the earth.

## A Prayer for the Fires in Australia

I have discovered that my attitude about tragedy is just a little off center. And I centered it. What do I mean by this? And how did this happen?

I recently attended a prayer for the fires in Australia. The event was held live by Rikka Zimmerman on Facebook. A man named Peter May joined her. I was live at this event in Ojai, California.

Many times, when there is a catastrophic event like the one that occurred in Australia, we go into the tragedy and misery of those who are suffering. We pray to end their suffering. But how do we pray for the earth? And the animals and then of course the people who are experiencing those events? What would truly benefit all concerned?

Do we pray for rain? Do we pray for the wind to change in certain areas so that the firefighters can combat the fires more easily? Do we pray for strength for the firefighters and to ease the suffering of all those who are there?

Rikka and Peter decided to speak with each of the elements. There is so much anger and frustration being thrown at the elements. Wind is hated. Trees and plants are seen as fostering the fire, and simultaneously seen experiencing their demise in the tragedy. Smoke is everywhere and it is choking. And people can't see. They just want the smoke to go away. They can't breathe.

> I look and I see the smoke as Godzilla. Misunderstood. Like a giant ape that climbs the empire state building and means no harm. But it makes people afraid of it.

But smoke is the alchemy of the earth.

> Water. May you rain down where you are most needed, and I thank you for your ability to give life and wash away the old.

We stand in the healing space of the animals and not in the tragedy of it.

> Thank you, animals, for being here and for being so brave.

And then we address the fire. What does the fire want? It just wants to be acknowledged.

*I see you fire. And I think of the warmth and nurturing of the fire in my fireplace back home.*

Peter plays the didgeridoo. We send our prayers through the vibrations of this Australian instrument through the ether to Australia where it is needed.

## A Little Girl Skips

*I see that I am a little girl of five or six skipping through and around the fires in Australia. I see all of them. I stop and look at them in awe and wonder. Then I skip on. I have no judgement. I just look in awe. I see the earth and I stop to pick up some soil, and I throw it into the air. It is caught on the wind, which blows it gently all over me. And I giggle with the dirt all over me. I see puddles and I stomp in them with my big red rubber boots, and I am so happy to be alive. I see smoke and I flitter it away and it dances with me and I giggle. I flick at the fire as though I am shooing a bug.*

I give the gift of this little girl who delights in all the elements. I give her to all. The elements, the readers, and even to those who are not yet ready to see her. She blows back at the wind with her little cheeks all puffed up and rosy. The elements were so tired of being fought. They just wanted a little peace and delight. They wanted the peace and delight of a child.

As stewards of the earth can we not give the elements that delight?

# Energy of Purpose

*There is a mystical person who is robed in white and has silver hair. She is dancing with her hands. I ask her if she pulled and pushed at the same time. She says as if talking to someone else, "Yes, she gets it." Then she slices through the air at her waist or near her heart. And I ask, "Did you cut through at your heart?" And she says, "Yes, she gets it." Then I fly alongside her, and she says, "Show-off!"*

*I know the dream is magical. We push and pull the energy and we go with the flow. The out push and pull directs the energy.*

Aligning and playing with the magic of energy is part of our purpose. Our Purpose is to experience the Magic of it. And to use that magic to align ourselves with the purity of our path.

## Sacred Technologies of Absolute Purpose

*Techniques for Purpose through Purpose*

1. **Answer** these questions:
   a. What makes your heart sing?
   b. What can you do for hours without stopping?
   c. What do others tell you that you are really good at?
2. **Choice.** Bring your heart into your mind. Take seven breaths. Sit in that place. Observe the infinite possibility around you. What do you choose?

*Techniques for Purpose through Joy*

3. **Magnificence of Everything.** Say three times, *By the law of divine grace and all that is light I* (state your name) *accept that everything is magnificent. Everything that I see is magnificent.*
4. **Magnificence of Self.** Say three times, *By the law of divine grace and all that is light I* (state your name) *accept that I am magnificent.*

*Techniques for Purpose through Love*

5. **Truth**. Say three times, *By the law of divine grace, and all that is light I* (state your name) *now accept that I choose from the space of the present moment.*

6. **Presence**: Be in gratitude for your breath. Thank your breath for supporting your life. Say, *thank you, breath.* Say this at least five times as you watch your breath. Do this several times during your day. Your breath brings you into the present moment. Choose from here.

*Techniques for Purpose through Peace*

7. **Kindness to Self.** Ask yourself, *Where could I be kinder with myself?* Do that.

8. **Kindness to Others.** Ask yourself how can you be kinder to your neighbor or a coworker. Do that.

9. **Bliss.** Let go of beliefs and of any definitions you have of Bliss. Allow whatever shows up. Show gratitude. Embrace it. Celebrate what shows up.

10. **Hoops of Color.** Relax your body. Ground it. Then run hoops of color up your body from your feet to your head. Envision the hoops as if they were hula hoops or large dream catchers with a fine mesh. Each hoop is a color of the corresponding chakra and the mesh of each one becomes more refined. Go from your feet up over your head. Add a couple of extra hoops that are pearlescent in pink, gold, and silver. When you are relaxed, grounded, and the energy is moving, say, *I am love, I am light, and I am infinite.* Then notice what happens.

*Techniques for Purpose through Intention*

11. **Gift to Others.** Ask yourself this question: *What gift can I give my readers, clients, or coworkers today?* Wait. Listen and then act.

12. **Gift to Self.** Ask yourself this question: *What gift can I give my body, mind, or spirit today?* Wait. Listen and then act.

# CHAPTER 12

# ABSOLUTE ENERGY

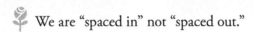 We are "spaced in" not "spaced out."

## Energy of Energy

*Meditation: Teaching Energy Weaving*

> *I am teaching energy weaving to a group. I start with recognizing energy and naming it because until you know who you are dancing with, you might not want to dance. Food and smells are a good place to start. I say, "This is the energy of rose. Smell the rose. This is the energy of the lemon. Smell the lemon." I explain: "When your mouth salivates at the suggestion, you know you are feeling the energy. When you can call that energy up at any time, then you are ready to dance with it."*
>
> *Then I move on to the energies of Peace, Love, and Joy.*
>
> *I start by feeling the energies that I know like Peace, Love, Joy, and ecstasy. I choose these because they are common, and I have already defined them for myself. It is easy for me to share their energies with the world.*
>
> *I start with the energy of Peace. It is calming and very blue. I feel and drink in its energy. I radiate out the blue energy of Peace to the group and then to the world.*

*I think about the polarity and divisiveness that exists in the world. I think about politics and the many protests that are going on around the world, in Iraq, France, Hong Kong, and the wars in the Ukraine. Not to mention the elections going on here and in the United Kingdom.*

*The earth seems angry. And she is reacting to what is happening on her surface. Covid-19 is spreading into every country on the planet. Swarms of locusts are spreading through parts of Africa. Killer wasps are entering the US from Canada.*

*But it is just energy. We can call the earth She and look at it that way. But we could also say the polar ice caps are melting and we have climate change and look at it that way. We could also say that it is energy. An equal and opposite reaction. So, what if we give her Peace? I stand and radiate all my Peace energy out to the world.*

*A huge ray, a bolt of lightning, comes down through me and into my heart and then goes into the hearts of all the members of the audience, and they radiate out and the energy flows out into the earth. And the earth says "Thank you. I needed that." And the earth takes a deep breath.*

*I save Love for last because it contains all energies and none at the same time.*

*So, I move on to Joy because it is full of movement and is my favorite. I use Joy energy to cleanse all other energies from my system. It's like a joy rinse. Then I choose ecstasy. It is very fast moving and can grow exponentially. I move to Bliss. I remind the audience that you don't have to go into a cave for months or years to experience it. You can just choose it. It is very refined. I start by holding it in a high place and then realize that I have to relax and let it flow through me. You cannot hold on to it. It too has to flow.*

*I end with Love. Love energy is nothing and everything at the same time. You can see infinite possibilities.*

*I decide to explore the energies of Rikka's Six Principles from here. I decide to hold and share the energy of each*

190

*principle. First is "Everything is made of love." But I think that if I begin with that, then there is nothing else. But I begin there anyway, and all five other principles are contained therein. Certainly the knowledge that "everything is made of infinite possibilities" is seen from this place. So, this is the energy of infinite possibility.*

*Then, "Everything is whole and complete." This is like the divine perfection that exists in this present moment, and I feel the energy of whole and complete.*

*And "already done" pops up. "Everything is already done." We are in the present moment where everything already exists and is already done. I take a breath as I relax into already done.*

*And then how about "everything is in support of and is supported by God." Life is easy when you accept this, and I feel the energy of easy and supported by God.*

*What about "everything and everyone is seen, heard, and acknowledged by God." What is the energy of that? It is the energy of communication and the dance of divine energy. It is the lead and the follow of the energy dance. The weave is the support and supported by.*

*And then there's the co-creation that flows from pure love and the allowance when we say yes.*

*Mastering Energy*

One way to master our lives is to master our Energy. We master energy by first recognizing the energy we are trying to master. By that I mean that we have to separate it from other energies and give it a name. Then we can dance with it. Once we can dance with it, then we can weave it. Weaving with it is the beginning of manifesting and creating with it. In order to do this, we need to be aware of the rules of energy.

## The Rules of Energy

We all have the ability to live our lives aligning with the rules of energy. We do so whether we are aware of the rules or not. Life is easier if we are aware of these rules. Matter is a kind of dense energy that flows, will not be contained, and emanates from source. Source is everywhere and nowhere at the same time, and matter is a reflection of the intent of source. Flow requires time and space, and in the absence of time and space nothing flows and yet everything flows in all directions from all points at the same eternal time. Energy is eternal and cannot be created or destroyed.

Knowing that these are the rules of energy, how do we then build our energy? Like the shamans and monks, we let go of self-importance, limiting beliefs, and judgements. We live in a world of experiences and we allow those experiences. We let go of the judgements we have about the experiences. Then we experience anew, and we allow. And then we let go of the judgement about each new experience. We repeat until we stand with Source at our back, in awe and wonder at all our experiences. Wonder dissolves the judgement.

## Infinity Ball

In my first book, *From Heartache to Joy*, I wrote about using the infinity symbol as an exercise to feel the energy of Harmony. The energy of yin and yang is surrounded by the energy symbol of a figure eight. Meditating on yin and yang as you move your hands around the infinity symbol brings you into the harmony of the universe. I used the following exercise

## Harmony

Move the energy in a figure eight, like the infinity symbol. Visualize the past to the left and the future to the right. The present is in the middle. Run the energy around it. See if you can spin the figure eight horizontally into a torus. See if you can spin the torus vertically so that it becomes a ball with a center point. All energy leads in and out at the same time. Play with it.

A few days ago, I was at a reunion class for Life Transformed Coaches. Rikka Zimmerman used a similar exercise to expand our beings into consciousness or space. She took the infinity symbol and ran her hands around it and then expanded it out. A couple of people had a difficult time with it because they saw it as two dimensional. After all, if you expand something only horizontally or vertically, it isn't infinite.

I thought of my exercise of going from a figure eight to a torus to a ball. I shared my exercise with Rikka and one of the students. Rikka said she got my ball when I was doing it and a member of the class thanked me for sharing my version because with that version she could expand out into the universe. She wasn't limited by two dimensions. It was already three dimensional.

I tried it with another person, and she had a difficult time with it. I had to walk her through it several times. Many people have a hard time with this exercise because it can be complicated to visualize.

This morning I thought about my infinity ball. I thought of going from the figure eight to the ball directly and it was so easy. Figure eight to ball. Boom. An infinity ball. No need to go through stages. Simply see an infinity ball. All energy moving around infinite figure eights and expanding out at the same time.

When time is present in the middle, past is on the left and future is on the right. But with the ball of figure eights, there is no left and right—past and future don't exist and the present moment is always expanding out.

 You give energy and receive it back ten times.

## Energy through Joy

What is the difference between the energy *of* Joy, and energy *through* Joy? Through Joy is about maintaining and increasing our Energy through Joy. We are not blocking or leaking our energy when we are Joyful. The Energy *of* Joy is about the Joy explosion I experienced in Bimini in 2016. It is about the billion sparkles of light that permeated my body when I asked to experience the Joy that God felt. Or probably more correctly stated as the energy that erupted out of my body as I now understand it.

When we are Joyful, we are in the position of allowing the energy to flow through us. We aren't blocking it. When blocked, the energy becomes stagnant like the water in a tidal pool. It doesn't go anywhere. And eventually it just leaks away. Joy allows us to both *not* leak our energy, and to build it and flow it. Joy is one of the higher energies. Apathy and struggle are lower energies. Hate is an intense energy, but it isn't very refined or high. We can grow our energy by playing in the Energy of Joy.

# Energy through Love

*The Energy of Love*

> *A dragonfly flitters by and lands on an elephant. Together they look down at the alligator lying in wait.*

In her poem, "How Do I Love Thee?" Elizabeth Barrett Browning said, "I love thee to the depth and breadth and height a soul can reach when feeling out of sight for the ends of being and ideal grace …. I love thee to the level of every day's most quiet need by sun and candle light."

I quoted her poem in my first book *From Heartache to Joy*, in the chapter on "Accessing Love." She so succinctly talks about what I am trying to explain. She puts the expression of Love into an art form while I am left explaining with a description of animal wisdoms.

Her line about "the depth and breadth and height a soul can reach when feeling out of sight for the ends of being and ideal grace" is absolute caring in the magnitude of presence. Or the wisdom of a dragonfly landing on an elephant looking down at an alligator.

*Human Love*

Love is all there is. I use my definition of Love this way. It is all things everywhere. *Human love* is less than that definition. But that is the way we usually think of love. I use a capital "L" for God's Love, and a small "l" for human love. The way a mother loves her baby, or we sometimes love a kitten or a puppy. The mature kind of love that I feel for my husband is a refined kind of love. But it is a kind of human love, and no matter how deeply it is felt, it is not the Love of God or the Universe, which is absolute allowance in all that we do, think, or say.

## Absolute Allowance

How can absolute allowance be? It is the energy of the Universe to explore and expand and evolve. We grow and expand and evolve with it. There has to be free will and total allowance for us to explore the possibilities. When we find a possibility that is evolutionary, we grow and expand. When we pick the wrong one, we become extinct like the dinosaur.

True Love is total allowance to pick and choose. The *ideal grace* part is found in the coming into alignment with evolution.

## Wisdom of the Animals

What is the wisdom of dragonfly? It flickers. It is quick. It barely touches down. Then it moves on. It is constantly in motion. Out over there and over there. Or how about over here? And here? Because it is landing on the magnitude of infinite possibility. And it is always doing it in the present moment. What is the wisdom of Elephant? *I am always here and I am very large. You can't make me go away and you can't move me. But you can sit on me.*

What about the wisdom of alligator? His mouth is always open, and he is looking up. The *presence* is always waiting.

The energy of Love contains all energies. It is the energy of total allowance. All the colors of the rainbow and all the colors that aren't even in the rainbow run through it. All feelings, all conditions, and all aspects. The human kind of love we feel is just one of the colors of love. It is a very good color. But still just one color. Love is the energy that exists before, during, and after all things that are really in the present moment.

# Energy through Abundance

*Preponderance*

> *An elephant joins me this morning. I'm not sure at first that I want to play with him. I see his little, tiny eyes looking out at me. And a small mouth smiling at me under his long trunk. I am reminded of a former experience with an elephant where I became one. It was so funny when I sneezed out his long nose and snot flew everywhere. It was hysterical. And then the trunk hung on throughout the day. I couldn't move my head without the trunk hitting me in the ears.*
>
> *I don't want a return to that experience. But he steps over to my right-hand side and stands there. He wraps his trunk around my back like a person putting their arm around your shoulder. Then he takes his left ear and puts it across and around my back. He holds me in his majesty. I think, "What now?" He stomps the floor with his massive foot and the room shakes. I think, "Hmmm. A preponderance of being. Huge energy and also kicking everything out of my way." In India, Ganesh moves everything out of your way, out of your path. Is elephant shaking the earth to tell them he and I are here?*

*Preponderance* is a funny word. It means weight or mass or supremacy. The elephant is all those things. The elephant showed me *preponderance*.

Words are just energy that are contained by their definitions. They are limiting but in a good way. They are like pictures. They freeze a meaning or event in time. They can change over time, like the word *cool*. Originally, it meant a cool temperature, and then it became something like *awesome* in meaning. So, words can change. But for a period of time, words limit and contain the energy of meaning.

Are words energy? Yes. They can soothe or crush. They can explain or muddle. Words are one way we share energy. Words have power. Be careful what you say. Or take care in what you say.

*Leaking Energy*

We all know those people who blather on. They are leaking their power with their words. Then there are those people who don't say anything. They are sometimes trying to hold on and contain their power. They are afraid. Power is an energy that cannot be contained and should not be leaked away. Power is something that should be directed with purpose. It does not have to be serious. It could be pointed at fun, ease, and Joy. It could be pointed at laughter. But it should be consciously directed.

*Save and Flow*

Energy should be saved, stored, flowed, and built up. Even though we are saving and storing, we are not containing it. We are still flowing it. We just aren't leaking it and not refilling the container. *Container.* Now that's not the right word. Because it means to contain. And the energy is meant to flow through us and energize us. It allows us to experience even greater events. Maybe *vessel* is the right word. It has two meanings. It can be a ship or a receptacle. I like that the energy is both in us and carrying us. Vessel is a better word. Our vessel that is our body can save, store, flow, and build up all at the same time. Yes! Elephant is an abundance (preponderance) of energy.

# Energy through Magic

What is the Energy of Magic? Do we gain energy through magic?

> *I think of Rikka with tiny fairies swirling around her. Fairy energy is so fast. It's just a flicker here and a flicker there. Many people can't see their energy because it is too fast. In order to be with them you have to speed your energy up or ask them to slow theirs down. I tell this to the group and tell them to ask the fairies to slow their energy down.*
>
> *There is a fairy for each member of the group. A tall, elven kind of fairy stands in front of me. Her speech is slow and understandable. Or have I just gotten very small and*

*fast? Whichever. I understand her. I tell the group to listen to the fairy on their shoulder. They have something to share with them. I ask my fairy what she has to say. "Speed up or slow down it doesn't matter. Size doesn't matter."*

*There is joy in the sparkle and twinkle of the fairy wings. And then they are gone. But not really. They flicker in and out. And they prick us with their tiny light sabers. "Wake up, wake up," they say. "Come and play in our world. Let us come and play in your world." And I wake up.*

We always gain energy when we allow and especially when we allow the mysterious energy of Magic. Want more energy? Allow more of the mysterious and the magical into your life.

## Energy through Intention

Aligning our intention with the intention of the universe both saves energy and gives us energy to flow toward our Intention. Intentionally practicing energy flow gives us the most energy.

### Reverse the Flow of your Breaths

This technique makes you aware of your breath and your energy field.

Breathe in and contract your energy field in. Visualize your energy coming in as you inhale and expanding out as you exhale. Expand it out several feet from your body. Do this in and out, synchronizing your breath and energy three times.

Then inhale and as you see it contracting inward, fall into that. Then expand it out even bigger. Out into the room you are in. Expand your energy field out and in with your breath. Do this three times.

Then expand out as big as your state and country and then the universe. Expand out into the universe and contract in into the Inverse that is inside of you. Do this three times. When you do this, you will notice that other people are also in your energy field. Whether in the room. Or in the world.

Yes, they are breathing also. You are breathing their energy and they are breathing yours.

Then reverse the breath and direction of expansion. Contract in on your outbreath and expand your energy out on your inbreath.

*Concertina Accordion Breath Number Two:*

If it seems hard to reverse the flow of energy with your breath, then think of the concertina, and expand your breath out when the concertina goes out and contract in when the concertina contracts. Breathe with the visualization of the concertina. See your breath as regulated by the air flow of the concertina going in and out. Use your hands playing the concertina to do this. Do this three times and then send your concertina breath out into the Universe and in, into the Universe (inverse) that is inside of you.

*Without Your Breath*

Now expand out into the Universe and in, into your inner Inverse without your breath. Just notice the expansion in and out. Notice it three times. Do this very slowly and deliberately. Then do it very quickly. Do it three times.

If you have a sticky or painful place in your body. Use that as the center point and operate your concertina breath from there. This technique will do several things—clean your energy field, get your energy moving, and make you aware of your energy and your breath.

# Energy through Divine Perfection

*The Hologram and Allowing*

We are all holograms. When I'm annoyed, I'm simply annoyed by someone else's hologram. I simply believed that someone else's simulation was my simulation. It isn't. They aren't. I wouldn't want to be them. But they can have their simulation. We are not less than or more than they are, because we are all holograms of God, we are all of it. We cannot be less than anyone else. A hologram is a complete copy of the whole from which it derives. If we are suffering, then everyone is also suffering.

In order to let go of all simulations from others say, *By the law of divine grace, I* (state your name) *ask that everyone else's simulation now leave.*

Also, let's save them from our own simulation. If they are running the same simulation, then it will leave. I rescue you if you will rescue me. I let go of that programming.

Say, *By the law of divine grace, I* (state your name) *ask that my own simulation now leave.*

## The Programmer

As I remember myself and stand with God (Universe), I am the programmer, not the programmed. I am the programmer of my hologram. The world will come to play in my world as I stand with God. Other individuals want to come home. They recognize their home as I stand with God. It's just your own energy trying to come back from a past that doesn't even exist.

In the present moment, there is no fear. If there is no fear, what is there to try to control? Belief in fear is mistrusting God. We are not a victim to the hologram of the world. It is just a bunch of simulations. These simulations are not our own. Say, *This simulation is not mine. It's not mine.*

So, how do I choose to see and experience? When I stand for the greater good, the whole world will change. I choose for the greater good.

Does the hologram have any feelings? Feelings are the biggest lie we've purchased. They are source energy that was put in the past to come forward.

## Space

Space shifts continuously and this creates energy. Perhaps "creates energy" is wrong, because energy can't be created. The shifting seems to create energy because the energy is intensified in one location instead of another. Space is natural, and energy wants to return to space. Being space is natural. It's always been space. I've always been space.

Say three times, *I've always been space.*

How much suffering do we endure about the density of our bodies? When you are not the programmer, it's dense. But your body is already space. It's already done. When we are not space, we are the programmed and not the programmer.

*But I am all energies*, we say. Yes, and we have graduated from being all energies.

Have you graduated from being all energies? Say three times, *I have graduated from being all energies.*

Everything is part of that space and there can be no separation. There is only the Glory of God, the Glory of Space. Space is the self-organizing balance and perfection. You don't have to do anything. It will organize itself and it is more efficient in its organization than we could ever be.

Can you run the organs of your own body? God is more efficient than we could ever be.

Space is so loving that God gave us free will. If we align with it, we are even more powerful.

Master space, not the energy of feelings. Enter into the space. Everything is here from space. Space is the unified field. Move into the space of being. There is no memory of where we just were.


*The Space Scape.*

What if this space is what we call Love? Space is infinitely in Love with you. It is an infinite landscape. Space is not distracted from loving you and me. It couples with the emotions to bring up the past. Space is without an explanation, because an explanation brings up the past, which is what we want to get rid of.

I don't know how, when, or where. I know that I am willing to accept that the space of God loves me and all that is.

*I accept. I accept. I accept.*

# Energy through Purpose

*Spaciousness*

A hologram has no energy in it. It is like a cartoon. What is real is the space surrounding it. We are not holding the space of Love or anything else. We are being the space. We are being one with the space. Is that just semantics? Is it really different being one with something from holding it? Yes, because if you are holding it, you're outside of it. You are separate from it. And that separation doesn't really exist. The action of being space activates the higher mind. Aren't the notions of action and being, doing and being funny? They are more like *becoming*, which has action and being at the same time. So, *becoming* activates the higher mind. While your higher mind orchestrates the body, the body is also in space, being space.

*The Mind*

The mind creates a filter between you and your body. Let go of that filter. Unravel it. Cancel it. Or just let it go. However, if you believe you can accomplish letting it go, do that.

Say, *In the name of God and all that is light, I* (state your name) *now let go of the need for my mind to filter my experiences.*

Tell yourself, *I am safe now. I don't need you to have any particular experience.*

Every projection, every thought, every belief, and every feeling become your filters.

Tell yourself, *I am a steward of my body.* Ask, *Body, how can I serve you?*

Thoughts are such heavy things. There is a constant bombardment of thoughts. Energy can't flow up. The thoughts are too heavy.

"Hello, earth." There's a level of projection in that. A projection into the earth. There is control in that projection also. Thank the earth. *Thank you, earth, for the space you hold. For the nurturing that you are. You can give the gift of the green elixir of the earth.*

*Consciousness Shift*

What is the global consciousness shift? The light being standing on the light being of earth. We are all connected light beings.

> *I see myself standing beside a child's sandbox. The sandbox is the earth. I see the emerald light of God. The turquoise light of the ocean. You are all me. I am the sky and the wind because I am blue. I am the gold of the sun. And I am connected to the earth at the same time. I am the silver light of the moon reflected on the water. I am the opalescent white light of infinite rainbows reflected in the drop of water on the leaf of the maple tree in front of my dining room window. The hologram is made up of that opalescent white.*

"Having dominion" is remembering the core true self. The God space recognizes the God space when we offer it. When the other sees this spaciousness, a part of him recognizes it and that part wants to join back up. Not realizing that it never really separated in the first place. Everything that we did before this was to get us to this place and this moment. All the unraveling and letting go. All the fixing and changing. Everything has led to this moment.

What is beyond energy mastery? Space Scapes. The final frontier! Ha! I am sorry for all the acts of separation that we have inflicted on the earth and all who stand on her. I am so sorry for all the acts of separation that I have inflicted on myself. I offer the divine space and release everything that the earth asks us for.

Hello. We have ended separation. We don't have to reflect any aspect of separation. Let all these reflections of separation go back to where they came from. This is Energy through Purpose. Aligning with the spaciousness of the Universe. Absolute Energy!

# Sacred Technologies of Absolute Energy

*Techniques for Energy through Energy*

1. **Figure of Eight.** Move the energy in a figure of eight, like the infinity symbol. Visualize the past to the left and the future to the right. The present is in the middle. Run the energy around it.
2. **Infinity Ball.** See if you can spin the figure eight horizontally into a torus. See if you can spin the torus vertically so that it becomes a ball with a center point. All energy leads in and out at the same time. Play with it.

*Techniques for Energy through Joy*

3. **The Elevator.** Imagine that you are in an elevator. You get on at the first floor, which is happy and maybe a little joyful. As you rise up through the floors each floor is increasingly more Joyful. When you get to the top, you get out. And then you notice that there is another elevator. And you ride this one to the top also. You get out. You can't possibly imagine that there is another elevator or any more Joy. But then you see another elevator.
4. **Waterfall and Geyser.** Imagine standing in a waterfall with all the opalescent colors of the rainbow falling down on you and washing into the earth. And then a geyser comes out of the earth and pushes all the colors of the rainbow up through your feet and out of your crown and into the heavens. And then the waterfall begins to rain down on you again and goes into the center of the earth. Run the energy of the waterfall down your spine. Hold your chakras back against your spine. Breathe in as the geyser rushes up and out as the waterfall runs down. Repeat this ten times.

*Techniques for Energy through Love:*

5. **Breath of God.** Imagine that God has sent an angel down to breathe with you. Imagine the angel standing in front of you with his wings out. He then reaches down with his face and

breathes out into your mouth. You breathe in. Then you breathe out and he breathes in. Soon you are breathing back and forth, with your outbreath being his inbreath and your inbreath being his outbreath. You do this for a while. Maybe five breaths.

Then the angel asks you if you want to breathe with God. You say yes. And a large gold trumpet appears where his mouth would be. Breathe in and out from this trumpet of God as you did with the angel. The air is very rarified. Do this several times.

Thank God and the angel for their breaths. They will thank you for your breath. Allow them to thank you.

6. **Breath of a Tree**. You can do the same exercise above but with a tree. Sit in front of a tree. Introduce yourself to it. And thank it for breathing your exhale. It breathes your carbon dioxide. If you listen, it will thank you for your breathing its oxygen. Then you and it can breathe each other consciously. You are doing it anyway. Repeat for ten minutes.

7. **Morning Prayer**. Say the Morning Prayer and end with this: "God, how much Love can I possibly be today? Show me how much Love I am. Show me how much you Love me." And then feel, listen, and watch. Watch throughout the rest of your day for signs of Love being reflected back at you. What are some examples of where Love is being demonstrated?

8. **Journaling:** Reflect in your journal on the following questions:
   - What did I see or feel during my Morning Prayer?
   - Where did I experience Love today?
   - Where did I give Love today?
   - Did I see Love where I never saw it before?
   - What color was it?
   - What did it smell like?
   - Does Love have a taste?
   - Where is Love located in my body?

*Techniques for Energy through Intent*

9. **Concertina Accordion Breath Number Two**: Do the same exercise as concertina accordion breath in chapter 6 but reverse the flow of your breaths.

10. **No Breath Accordion.** Do the same exercise without your breath that you performed in the concertina accordion breath. Expand in and out without your breath.

*Techniques for Energy through Divine Perfection*

11. **Not My Simulation.** Say three times, *In the name of God and by the law of divine grace, I* (state your name) *ask that everyone else's simulation now leave.*

12. **Simulation Now Leave**. Say three times, *By the law of divine grace, I* (state your name) *ask that my own simulation now leave.*

13. **I Am Space.** Say three times, *By the law of divine grace, I* (state your name) *accept that I've always been space.*

*Techniques for Energy through Purpose*

14. **Mind as Filter.** Say, *In the name of God and all that is light, I* (state your name) *now let go of the need for my mind to filter my experiences.*

15. **Safety.** Say, *In the name of God and all that is light, I* (state your name) *am safe now. I don't need myself to have any particular experience.*

16. **Steward of Body.** Say, *In the name of God and all that is light, I* (state your name) *am a steward of my body. Body, how can I serve you?*

17. **Reflections Back.** Say, *In the name of God and all that is light, I* (state your name) *now let all these reflections go back to where they came from.*

18. **No Out or In.** Find your center and then expand out four or five feet. Then expand out to the room; then the city; then the state;

then the country; then the earth, and then the universe. Or just expand out as big as the universe. Try the reverse and expand or fall into the center that is you. Then further in and further in until there is no in or out. You just are. You are space.

# CHAPTER 13

# SACRED TECHNOLOGIES OF THE ABSOLUTE

 The techniques exercise us. They move us.

I call these *sacred* technologies because they are connected to God, the Universe, Source, Force, and Energy. And they can work. If you have seen any of them before, and tried them, try them again. You are not the same person you were last year or even an hour ago. If when you try a technique, it doesn't seem to work or you don't like it, move on to the next one. Try one that seems right for you. Don't force yourself but do give yourself the opportunity to at least take a taste. When we practice, we gain experience. We need to let experience be our advisor.

Not all of the techniques are referenced in the chapter. Sometimes I have simply added them because I believe they would be useful for energizing a particular aspect.

I came to each of the chapters, pathways, aspects, conditions, and tools one at a time. I practiced each for several weeks and even months. I practiced the same aspect like Peace for several months before I heard the next word, which was Love. Each word came to me after a long practice of the previous word or pathway. Then I began to combine them as I have done here. Practice them alone before you explore them together. Practice each one alone or together in the Morning Prayer. And try the rest of the sacred technologies.

# Chapter 1 ~ The Absolute

*Sacred Technologies of the Absolute*

1. **No Matter What.** Say: *No matter what, I am absolute …* (fill in the blank with an energy like Joy, Peace, or Love). You can also say, *No matter what I am*, and then say nothing. That is even more absolutely absolute.
2. **Morning Prayer**. Pick one word for the day, and look for that aspect, condition, or tool throughout your day.
3. **Align** yourself with the day's word. The word will align you with your path. Check throughout your day. Are you still noticing that word?
4. **Choose**. Say three times: *I now choose to stay on my path, no matter what.*
5. **Centering.** Focus on your breath. Be grateful for your breath. Breathe in and out ten times counting to seven on the in and the out breaths. Make your breath circular. Do not hold it in at the top or the bottom of your breath. Focus on your breath and nothing else.
6. **Focus**. Notice your noticing. Play with focus and fuzzy awareness within the act of noticing. Go from laser focus to fuzzy awareness. Go back and forth. Can you do both at the same time? What are you noticing right now?

# Chapter 2 ~ Absolute Joy

*Techniques for Joy through Peace*

1. **Dissolve Negative Energies**. Stand in the energy that is the opposite of the negative energy. If you are confronted with hate, stand in love; in fear, stand in courage; in struggle, stand in peace. Do not engage the other person in conflict. Allow them to have their feeling, until they don't. Say, *I'm sorry you hate that so. I know that must be painful. I don't hate it.*

## *Techniques for Joy through Magic*

2. **Bless Your Food** with a sprinkle of magic dust. Also do this with coffee and water.
3. **Bless Other People** and your family with magic dust. Do it with or without them being aware of it. Wish them well and give them Joy. You can also bless strangers on the street.
4. **Bless Yourself** with magic dust. Sprinkle it on yourself. Give yourself Joy.

## *Techniques for Joy through Divine Perfection*

5. **Energy of Joy.** Ask the universe to show you what Joy feels like.
6. **Energy of Divine Perfection.** Ask the universe to show you what Divine Perfection feels like.
7. **Joy through Divine Perfection.** Ask the universe to show you the Joy in Divine Perfection. What does that feel like?
8. **Accept Divine Perfection.** Say three times, *I* (state your name) *now accept the dance of Divine Perfection.*
9. **Dance Divine Perfection.** Say three times, *I* (state your name) *will now dance the dance of Divine Perfection with Joy.*

## *Techniques for Joy through Purpose*

10. **Color of the Path**. Ask the universe to show you your right path by showing you a color.
11. **Recognition**. Ask the universe how you can recognize the correct path for your purpose.
12. **Joyful Path.** Ask if this path is bringing you Joy.
13. **Laugh** for no reason.

# Chapter 3 ~ Absolute Peace

*Techniques for Feeling Peace through Joy*

1. **Let Go of Struggling**. Let go of struggling with whatever you are doing. Stop. Take a few deep breaths. Look around you. Be grateful for being here. Choose to participate in what you are doing from *That's interesting.* Or *That's fun* or *That's …* fill in the blanks with something other than struggle.

2. **Choice.** Say three times, *I choose to let go of the idea of struggle. I choose easy. I choose fun. I choose ….*

3. **How Easy?** Ask three times, *I wonder how easy this could possibly be?* Then wait and watch.

*Technique for Peace through Love*

4. **Love Anyway.** When you are in a situation where you don't agree with a person's action, separate their behavior from the person. You don't have to like their actions. But you have to like the person. Love them anyway.

*Techniques for Peace through Health*

5. **Glowing Health.** Ask yourself, *What does wellness feel like? What does health feel like?* Bring that feeling into the part of your life that is struggling. See health as glowing and vigorous. Then bring glowing and vigorous into your wealth or your relationship. Bring it where you need it. Bring it to wherever you struggle.

6. **Cell Ease.** Ask yourself what does Peace feel like? Bring that sense of ease and already done into your body. Bring it into the part of your body that is distressing you. Bring it into every cell of your body.

*Techniques for Peace through Gratitude*

7. **Seven Seconds Breathing.** Breathe in for seven seconds and out for seven seconds. Do this five times. This will calm you.

8. **Let go of Belief.** Let go of the belief that you are controlled by your past. Say three times. *By the law of divine grace and all that is light, I* (state your name) *let go of the belief that my past controls my present. I am here now.*

9. **Grateful.** Say three times, *By the law of divine grace and all that is light, I* (state your name) *am grateful for the situation I am in right now. Thank you. Thank you. Thank you.*

*Techniques for Peace through Intention*

10. **Dissipate the Energy.** Take seven steps forward. Turn around. Look at where you were standing. Dissipate the energy where you were standing. Watch it dissipate. Wave your fingers at it and tell it to dissipate.

11. **Existing Peace.** Make a list of where you already see Peace in your life. Write the list down. Do this every day for one week.

*Techniques for Peace through Divine Perfection*

12. **Encode with Peace.** Say three times, *I now know that all products are encoded with energy. I choose those products that are encoded with Peace.*

13. **Accept No Change**. Say three times, *I accept who I already am. I accept the change of no change.*

14. **Tapping**. Say three times as you tap your forehead, *I tap my forehead with the blessing of Divine Perfection.*

*Techniques for Peace through Energy*

15. **Peace Energy.** Ask to be shown what the energy of Peace feels like. What color is it? What does it smell or taste like?

# Chapter 4 ~ Absolute Love

*Techniques for Love through Health*

1. **Thank Your Body.** When your body seems to get well on its own or with your help, say, *Thank you, body, for healing yourself.* Say, *Thank you. Thank you. Thank you.*
2. **Behavioral Awareness.** When you get sick and it seems to be the result of some behavior, say, *Thank you, body, for making me aware of my behavior. I will do better next time. I will take better care of you next time. Thank you. Thank you. Thank you.*

*Techniques for Love through Gratitude.*

3. **Gratitude for Your Partner.** Say three times, *Thank you for the wonderful partner I have. Thank you. Thank you. Thank you.*
4. **Gratitude for Your Friend.** Say three times, *Thank you for my best friend, …* (fill in the blank.) *Thank you. Thank you. Thank you.*
5. **Gratitude for Your Family Members**. Say three times. *Thank you for my loving family.* (Say this even if they haven't been so loving in the past.) *Thank you. Thank you. Thank you.*
6. **Gratitude for Life.** Say three times, *Thank you for the wonderful life I have. Thank you. Thank you. Thank you.*

*Technique for Love through Magic*

7. **What Else?** Think about a situation or relationship that you would like to add some love to. Ask, *What else might I know about this? What else is there?* Listen.

*Techniques for Love through Intention*

8. **Rheostat.** Create a rheostat for *yes.* Turn it on, and turn up the intensity. You can also turn it down when you don't need as much energy. Keep your *yes* running on low.

*Techniques for Love through Presence*

9. **Presence.** When you find yourself going into worry or anxiety, come back to the present moment. Remember the future does not exist. Only the present moment exists.

*Techniques for Love through Energy*

10. **Volleyball.** Play energetic volleyball with someone. Put the love of your heart into it, and pass it back and forth.

# Chapter 5 ~ Absolute Abundance

*Techniques for Abundance through Love*

1. **Gratitude for What Is**. Say, *Thank you, Universe, for the abundance that is already in my life. Thank you. Thank you. Thank you.*
2. **Gratitude for the Future**. Say, *Thank you, Universe, for the abundance I am about to receive.*
3. **Celebrate**. Let go of wanting. Celebrate what you have. Sing and dance in that celebration.

*Techniques for Abundance through Joy*

4. **Heartfelt Gratitude.** Place your hand over your heart and feel the gratitude as you say *Thank you for …* (fill in the blank with what you already have).
5. **Relationship with Money.** Treat your money as if you were in a relationship with it. Because you are. Allow it to be whatever it wants to be and love and be joyful with it anyway. Say, *I love you anyway, money.*
6. **Whatever Way.** Then love your money however it wants to show up. Say, *Thank you for …* every time, in whatever way it shows up.

*Techniques for Abundance through Health*

7. **Day Off.** Take a day off. Do something different. Rest and Play. Whatever that means to you. Do this at least once a month.

*Techniques for Abundance through Gratitude*

8. **Past Abundance.** Make a list of all the ways you have received abundance in the past. Give gratitude for each of these things on your list.
9. **Current Abundance.** Make a list. Where do you currently see abundance around you? Give gratitude for each of these things on your list.

*Techniques for Abundance through Purpose*

10. **Listen for Purpose.** Ask what your purpose is. Say, *Universe, what is my purpose?* And then listen.
11. **Accept.** Say, *I* (state your name) *now accept that my purpose is ....*
12. **Alignment Button.** Align your purpose with the intent of the universe. Imagine that you have an alignment button on the dashboard in front of you. Hit that button and say, *I* (state your name) *now align my intention with the intention of the Universe.*

*Technique for Abundance through Energy*

13. **Energy of Abundance.** Ask the Universe to show you what Abundance feels like. Does it have a color or a taste or a smell?

# Chapter 6 ~ Absolute Health

*Techniques for Health through Love*

1. **Increase Receiving**. Say three times, *I now choose to receive ...* (insert *Love, health* or *wealth*). Say whatever you would like to receive. You could also say, *I choose to receive receiving.*
2. **Receiving Breath.** Breathe in slowly and out slowly as you count to seven seconds. Do this seven times. Feel the energy of receiving as you inhale and feel yourself letting go as you exhale.

*Techniques for Health through Peace*

3. **Food Awareness.** Eat your food with the intention of nourishing your body. Eat with the intent of pleasure. Ask God what the food tastes like. Listen with your awareness.
4. **Wonder.** Ask yourself how a plant or a tree feels. Do they have peace or Joy or beauty or abundance or power? What is it that the plant reflects in you?
5. **Expand Your Energy** in and out. Shrink your energy field in as small as you can make it into your center. Then expand it out as big as the Universe. Coordinate its expansion and contraction with your inbreaths and outbreaths. Don't just contract in to your normal size of energy field. Contract your energy into a center that goes in as far as the Universe goes out. Now that's really falling into yourself!
6. **Cocoon.** Once you have your energy moving with the in-and-out exercise above, unzip the front of your energy cocoon and step out.
7. **Let Go of Another's Energy.** Say, *Everything that doesn't belong to me, now leave.* And then fill the space with gratitude. Say, *I wonder how much gratitude I can feel.*
8. **Wonder.** Ask yourself, *How much can I Wonder? What does Wonder feel like?*
9. **Mirror Work.** Look in a mirror. Tell yourself that you are beautiful. Find something that you can believe. If you like your hair, tell yourself that you have beautiful hair. Do this for a few

minutes. Do this every day. Then change to something else that you find beautiful. As you do this more often, what you see as beautiful will change. Do this every day. Maybe as you brush your teeth.

10. **A Place of Beauty**. Sit in a place of exquisite beauty or listen to music of exquisite beauty. Ask it why it is so beautiful. And listen to the answer. Know that it is only the reflection of your own exquisite beauty. Then ask yourself how you feel.

11. **Structured Water Flow**. Flow energy down your spine as if you were a huge tube, as if you were a structured water filter. Send the energy across each chakra, where you have placed a ball. Swirl the energy around those balls clockwise and counterclockwise. Start the energy at your heart chakra and send the energy out and around in all directions. Work your way up and down your chakras. This exercise will get your energy flowing. Do at least three times.

12. **Triangle Energy.** Move your energy in a triangle. Open your palms and see the sun above your head, and your mind and spirit in your palms. Circulate the energy around the triangle. The apex is the sun energy. Your right hand is your mind energy. Your left hand is your spirit or heart energy. Move the energy around the triangle in one direction and then in the other. Do at least three times. This will get your energy moving. It will also put your heart in your mind and your mind in your heart or spirit.

13. **Connect Health to Breath**. Breathe in and out slowly as you count to seven seconds. Do this seven times. Feel the energy of perfect health as you inhale and feel yourself letting go of dis-ease as you exhale.

14. **Yogic Breathing**: Try breathing in through your nose for a count of eight, hold for six seconds and breathe out through your nose for a count of six. Hold out for a count of four. Repeat ten times.

15. **Conscious Breathing** (the circular breath) Pull the breath in through your mouth and let it drop out very quickly. Don't push it out. There is no pause at the top or bottom of the breath. Do this for fifteen breaths or for ten minutes. Ask a question about your health. Listen for the answer. Journal or meditate about it.

16. **Breathing Expert.** Find a conscious breathing expert near you. There are now many breathing experts who practice online. You can try one of those.

17. **Breathe the Magnificence.** Look at something you believe is magnificent. Like a sunrise, sunset, the ocean, or a tree. Breathe in its magnificence. Sit with it for 10 minutes. Journal or meditate on it.

18. **Focus on Magnificence.** Look to see the magnificence in the world. Be aware of but let go of anything you think is junk. Put the junk in your peripheral vision and put your focus on magnificence.

19. **Concertina Accordion Breath.** Breathe in and out like a concertina accordion going in and out. Pretend that you are holding a small six-inch-by-six-inch concertina accordion in your hands. Breathe in and out with it as you pull and push the concertina in and out. Do this until your breath is in harmony with the action of the concertina. Then place the concertina over some part of your body that has a pain. Like your knee. Breathe in and out as you play your imaginary concertina over and through your knee. Let the concertina breathe your knee. Let your knee breathe the concertina. Try it with any part of your body that hurts. Do this for five minutes. (See further instructions for this practice at heartachetojoy.com/accordion-breath.)

20. **Breathing the Chakras.** Take a deep breath and feel who you are, and then take a deep breath into each chakra starting at the root and working your way up to the crown chakra to discover what each chakra's energy is. Then breathe yourself and breathe that chakra until you and it are not separate. You are the same. Do this with each chakra and then move on to the next one.

21. **Breathe a Gemstone.** Use the same technique as you used in breathing the chakras. Breathe yourself and breathe the gemstone until you merge.

22. **Feel, Breathe, and Release.** Try seeing a negative feeling such as anger or sadness through the lens of divinity and awareness. First, you feel it. Then you take a deep breath and let it go.

23. **Breathe the Breath of God.** Breathe yourself and then breathe God. Do this until there is only one of you.

24. **Expanding in**. Practice expanding yourself into the core of your being on your inbreath and expand out to normal size on your outbreath. Then reverse the inbreaths and outbreaths with the practice.
25. **Internal Source Point.** Practice breathing your internal source point. Breathe while you focus your attention on your center.

*Techniques for Health through Gratitude*

26. **Past Health.** Say three times, *Thank you, Universe, for my past good health. Thank you, thank you, thank you.*
27. **Find Something Healthy.** Say three times, *Thank you, Universe, for my healthy* ... (fill in the blank).
28. **Allow.** Say three times, *Thank you, Universe, for the perfect health that I already have.*

*Techniques for Health through Intention*

29. **See Beauty** in all things. Tell everything that you see that it is beautiful. Look around you and for ten minutes tell everything that it is beautiful.
30. **Most Beautiful.** List the ten most beautiful things that you saw today.
31. **Tell Another**. Tell another person how beautiful they are. In person or in writing.
32. **Allow Beauty.** Allow your own beauty to shine forth. Your beauty will heal all those around you. Say, *By the law of divine grace and all that is light, I now allow my own beauty to shine forth.*
33. **Accept Beauty.** Say, *By the law of divine grace and all that is light, I* (state your name) *now accept the beauty that I am.*
34. **A Reflection.** Say, *By the law of divine grace and all that is light, I* (state your name) *accept that the beauty that others see in me is only the reflection of their own beauty.*

*Techniques for Health through Purpose*

35. **Choice.** Say three times, *By the law of divine grace and all that is light, I* (state your name) *now choose perfect health.*
36. **Listen.** Say three times, *By the law of divine grace and all that is light, I* (state your name) *listen to my body.*
37. **Conscious Choice.** Say three times, *By the law of divine grace and all that is light, I* (state your name) *make conscious and informed choices about my health.*

# Chapter 7 ~ Absolute Gratitude

*Techniques for Gratitude through Gratitude*

1. **Resistance to an Event.** Say three times, *In the name of God and all that is light, I* (state your name) *let go of my resistance to this event.* (State what the event is.)
2. **Acceptance of an Event.** Say three times, *In the name of God and all that is light, I* (state your name) *accept this event.* (State what the event is.)
3. **Give Thanks for an Event.** Say three times, *In the name of God and all that is light, I* (state your name) *give thanks for this event.* (State what the event is.) *Thank you. Thank you. Thank you.*
4. **Celebrate an Event.** Say three times, *In the name of God and all that is light, I* (state your name) *celebrate the lessons I have learned. Thank you. Thank you. Thank you.* (Replace *lesson* with freedom or power or with whatever lesson you ad.)

*Techniques for Gratitude through Joy*

5. **Gratitude for Breath**. Take seven complete deep breaths. With each breath, say, *Thank you for this breath. Thank you for this clean air.*
6. **Joyful Condition.** Think of something you are joyful about. Give thanks for it. Say thank you three times.

7. **Gratitude for Easy.** When you begin a project. Thank the Universe for its successful outcome before you have even started. Say, *Thank you for this project being so easy and so successful.* Put it in your own words. And see how easy it becomes.

*Techniques for Gratitude through Abundance*

8. **Abundance Everywhere.** Say three times, *Thank you for the abundance that exists everywhere. Thank you. Thank you. Thank you.*
9. **Abundant Condition.** Say three times, *Thank you for the abundant* … (fill in the blank). *Thank you. Thank you. Thank you.*
10. **Abundant Experience.** Say three times, *Thank you for the abundance of the experiences that fill my day. Thank you. Thank you. Thank you.*

*Techniques for Gratitude through Peace*

11. **Easy.** Ask what is the best and easiest way to do this? Listen for the answer.
12. **Easy life.** *I* (state your name) *accept that my life is easy.*
13. **Gratitude for Ease.** *I* (state your name) *am grateful that my life is easy. Thank you, thank you, thank you.*

*Techniques: for Gratitude through Purpose*

14. **Resistance to Glory.** Say three times, *In the name of God and all that is light, I* (state your name) *let go of my resistance to the Glory of God (the Universe).*
15. **Accept Glory.** Say three times, *In the name of God and all that is light, I* (state your name) *accept the Glory of God.*
16. **Step into Glory.** Say three times, *In the name of God and all that is light, I* (state your name) *step into the glory of God in all my being and doing.*

17. **Celebrate Glory.** Say three times, *In the name of God and all that is light, I* (state your name) *celebrate the Glory of God in my "beauty."* (Replace *beauty* with whatever you are resisting.)

18. **Wisdom**. Listen. Be in silence for one hour, half a day, or a full day. Do not speak. Just listen. Listen to the plants and animals. Listen to the silence. Do this as often as you can.

# Chapter 8 ~ Absolute Magic

*Techniques for Magic through Magic*

1. **Bring your Heart into your Mind** or your mind into your heart. Both work. Do the one that seems easier to you. Breathe. Reach up into the highest vibration that you can find. Breathe. Reach down into the center of the earth. Breathe. Do this three times. Then find your center at your heart and bring your mind down into your heart. Let your awareness expand out from this state. You will find that you act in Peace.

2. **Watch your Mind.** Give your mind some activity to work on. Then let it go and don't think about it. Just watch it being busy.

3. **Presence.** Step into the present moment. Watch your breath. Take seven in and out breaths. Let go of any attachments to the past. Let go of any anxiety about the future. Look around you. What do you see right now? What is here? Now, what would you like to do?

*Techniques for Magic through Joy*

4. **Transform into Joy.** Say three times, *I now accept that anything in my life that isn't joyful can be transformed into Joy.*

5. **Magic of Transformation.** Say three times, *I now accept the Magic of transformation.*

*Techniques for Magic through Abundance*

6. **Infinitely Abundant.** Say, *I* (state your name) *believe in an infinitely abundant Universe.*

7. **Magical Universe.** Say, *I* (state your name) *believe that the Universe is magical.*

*Techniques for Magic through Peace*

8. **Breath of Peace**. Do seven-second breathing. Watch your breath. Breath in for seven seconds and out for seven seconds. Do this seven times. Then speak or take action.

9. **Decide to Be Right or to Be Peaceful.** The next time you enter into a confrontation, ask yourself, *Do I want to be right or do I want to be happy and in Peace?* State your opinion and then let it go.

10. **Power and Lightness.** Practice the exercise for power and lightness. Play with the lightness. Play with power. Combine the two. Send the lightest wisp of energy like a feather down into the earth and then up into the sky. How light a wisp can you send up into the sky and still feel its energy? Then reverse the process. Send the energy of an atomic bomb down into the earth and then up into the sky. How was that? Place the power of the atomic bomb into the lightness of the feather and then send it down into the earth and then up into the sky? How was that? Practice doing them separately and then together.

*Techniques for Magic through Divine Perfection*

11. **Past Magic.** List all the magical occurrences you have seen in your life.

12. **Past Cosmic Coincidences.** List all the cosmic coincidences you have seen in your life.

13. **Current Magic.** List all the magic that occurred yesterday.

14. **All Is Magic.** Say three times, *In the name of God and all that is light, by the law of divine grace, I* (state your name) *accept that all of life is Magic.*

*Techniques for Magic through Purpose*

15. **Step into Magnificence.** Say three times, *In the name of God and all that is light, by the law of divine grace, I* (state your name) *now choose to step into the magnificence of all that is.*

16. **Choose to Shine.** Say three times, *In the name of God and all that is light, by the law of divine grace, I* (state your name) *choose to shine forth my light.*

17. **Align with Love.** Say three times, *In the name of God and all that is light, by the law of divine grace, I* (state your name) *choose to align with the love of the Universe.*

18. **Conscious Intelligence.** Say three times, *In the name of God and all that is light, by the law of divine grace, I* (state your name) *choose to align with the conscious intelligence of the Universe.*

19. **Stand in Love and Cooperation.** Say three times, *In the name of God and all that is light, by the law of divine grace, I* (state your name) *choose to stand in love and cooperation with the Universe.*

20. **Already Done.** Say three times, *In the name of God and all that is light, by the law of divine grace, I* (state your name) *accept that it is already done.*

*Techniques for Magic through Energy*

21. **Seven Chakras.** Run through the seven chakras as explained in the chapter. Ask what color and what smell and what taste each one has for you.

22. **Experience the Energy of Magic.** Ask to be shown the energy of Magic. Say, *Universe will you show me what the energy of Magic looks like? Tastes like? Smells like? And feels like?*

# Chapter 9 ~ Absolute Co-creation

*Techniques for Co-creation through Intention*

1. **Grounding through Your Feet**. Feel into the earth with the energy of your feet. Tickle the center of the earth. Take a deep

breath. Imagine that you have copper strands from the bottom of your feet going way down to the center of the earth. Watch and allow as the copper tendrils conduct the earth energy up into your feet, and then allow it to go up into your heart and out through your crown. Do this three times.

2. **Grounding through Your Knees**. For grounding into the earth with the energy of your knees, watch as you send silver strands of energy down into the earth from your knees. See yourself as a silver being standing on a silver energy field that is at the top of several hundred feet of silver soil. All is silver, and it spreads out horizontally across the earth. Stay in this place for several breaths.

3. **Clairsentience from the Heart.** For feeling, go into your heart. Expand out as big as the universe. Ask your heart what it knows about this. Ask all of your questions from this place. This is learning to know from the place of feeling awareness.

4. **Claircognizance from the Heart-Mind.** Join your heart with your mind. Bring your mind down into your heart. Or you can bring your heart up into your mind. Reside there. From this place ask a question and step into the answer. Feel into it with your heart-mind or allow it to pop up. Communicate from this place of knowing awareness.

5. **Morning Prayer**. Pick one word for the day and look for that aspect, condition, or tool throughout your day.

6. **Align.** Align yourself with that aspect. It will align you with your path. Check throughout your day. Are you still noticing that word?

7. **No Matter What.** Say three times, *I now choose to stay on my path, no matter what.*

*Techniques for Co-Creation through Joy*

8. **Grace toward Others.** *I* (state your name) *acknowledge that I will speak and act in grace with kindness to others in all that I say and do.*

9. **Grace toward Self**. *I* (state your name) *acknowledge that I will act in grace with kindness to myself.*

10. **Allow Others.** *I* (state your name) *acknowledge that I will listen to the ideas of others. I will allow them to have their own ideas.*

11. **Respect Self.** *I* (state your name) *acknowledge that I will respect myself in everything that I do and say.*
12. **Respect Others.** *I* (state your name) *acknowledge that I will respect others in all that they do and say.*

### *Techniques for Co-Creation through Love*

13. **Yes to the Universe.** Say three times, *I* (state your name) *now accept that I Co-Create with the Universe. I say* Yes *to the universe.*
14. **Yes to Myself.** Say three times, *I* (state your name) *now say* Yes *to myself.*

### *Techniques for Co-Creation through Divine Perfection*

15. **Noticing.** Increase your ability to notice. Notice what is in front of you. Then ask, *What else is there about this? What else might I notice?*
16. **Categories.** Make a list of the things you would like to change in your life. Determine which category or categories they fall into— life, health, love, spirituality, or Abundance. Do you have more than one category? Pick one to focus on.
17. **Ask for Help.** Ask the universe to bring into your life the right class, book, or person to help with that change. Notice when that help shows up. Take action. Your action is aligning yourself with the Universe.

### *Technique for Co-Creation through Purpose*

18. **Focus and Awareness.** Come into the present moment. Look at something. Then allow your eyes to go soft and see all around you even in the back of your head. This is awareness. Now go back to focus. Keep your focus straight ahead. Go back and forth from focus to fuzzy awareness. Do this several times. Eventually you will realize that you are doing both at the same time.

*Technique for Co-Creation through Energy*

19. **Over There.** Pick any spot. See yourself as an energetic body "over there." An energy being. Full of light. Pull it back. Send it out and pull it back. Do this several times. When you are comfortable, have the energy being turn around and see an energy being where you are currently standing. And then pull the energy back to "over there." Now the awareness of your current location has become the "over there." See the "now here" from over there. Pull the energy back to where you are standing. In which location are you? Which have you chosen? Remember when you are done to always pull all your energy back to you. You don't want to leave it sprinkled around the universe. Do this only to the degree that you are comfortable. It should be fun.

# Chapter 10 ~ Absolute Divine Perfection

*Techniques for Divine Perfection through Love:*

1. **Past Incidences.** Make a list of the incidences that occurred in the past that you might have thought were bad but then turned out to be for the better.
2. **Today's Incidences.** List the incidents of divine perfection that occurred that day. Try to notice ten. Do this for one week.
3. **Morning Prayer.** Ask God to show you what Divine Perfection looks like.
4. **Early Morning.** When you get up in the morning, say, *I wonder what wondrous, magical thing will happen **today**.* Then Notice it. Then watch it happen. Give gratitude when it does. The more you do this, the more you notice the magical things that are already happening around you.
5. **Throughout the Day.** Repeat as often as you can remember to throughout the day, *I wonder what wondrous, magical thing will happen **next**?* Then watch it happen. Give gratitude when it does.

*Techniques for Divine Perfection through Peace*

6. **I am love. You are love.** Say, *I am love. I am light. I am infinite.* Say, *You are love. You are light. You are infinite.* Say each three times. Notice the difference. Where does each phrase reside in you? Bring the two locations together into one source point and say the phrases again.

7. **Moving Meditation.** Use the above phrase as a walking meditation. Say, *I am love. I am light. I am infinite.* Say, *You are love. You are light. You are infinite.* I use it on each step I take or each stroke I swim. What this exercise does is it allows you to embody the statement. It embodies *I am love.*

8. **Create an Alignment Button**. Notice which direction your spirit is going in. Create an alignment button on your spiritual computer. Then hit your alignment button. When you align with your spirit, you act in Peace.

9. **Say the Morning Prayer** and ask to be shown what Peace feels like. Ask God to show you the Peace that surrounds you in life. Notice where it appears in the rest of your day.

10. **Reflect** in your journal on the following questions:
    - What did you see or feel during your Morning Prayer?
    - Where did you experience Peace today?
    - Where did you align with spirit today?
    - Did you see Peace where you had never seen it before?
    - What color was it?
    - What did it smell like?
    - Does Peace have a taste?
    - Where is Peace located in my body?

*Techniques for Divine Perfection through Intention*

11. **Not Bad but Good.** Make a list of past incidents that you thought were bad but then turned out to be for the best.

12. **Incidents of Divine Perfection.** List the incidents of Divine Perfection that occurred today or this week or month or year

when something happened that you thought was bad and turned out to be for the best. Try to notice ten.

13. **Cosmic Coincidences.** List the incidents of cosmic coincidences that occurred today. Try to notice ten. Do this for one week.

14. **Morning Prayer.** Ask God to show you what Divine Perfection looks like.

## *Journaling*

15. Reflect in your journal on the following questions:
    - What did I see or feel during my Morning Prayer?
    - Where did I experience Divine Perfection today?
    - Where did I align with Divine Perfection today?
    - Did I see Divine Perfection where I had never seen it before?
    - What color was it?
    - What did it smell like?
    - Does Divine Perfection have a taste?
    - Where is Divine Perfection located in my body?

## *Technique for Divine Perfection through Purpose*

16. **Already Whole.** Say three times, *I am already whole and complete.*

17. **No Fixing.** Say three times, *There is no need for fixing and changing.*

18. **Acceptance.** Say three times, *I accept what is. It is okay. It is better than okay.*

19. **My Purpose.** Say three times, *As I step into a new world, I step into my purpose.*

20. **New World.** Say three times, *The new world is my purpose.*

## *Techniques for Divine Perfection through Energy*

21. **Synchronicity Energy.** Ask, *What does synchronicity feel like?* Then feel it.

22. **Divine Perfection Energy.** Ask, *What does Divine Perfection feel like?* Then feel it.

# Chapter 11 ~ Absolute Purpose

*Techniques for Purpose through Purpose*

1. **Answer** these questions:
   a. What makes your heart sing?
   b. What can you do for hours without stopping?
   c. What do others tell you that you are really good at?
2. **Choice.** Bring your heart into your mind. Take seven breaths. Sit in that place. Observe the infinite possibility around you. What do you choose?

*Techniques for Purpose through Joy*

3. **Magnificence of Everything.** Say three times, *By the law of divine grace and all that is light I* (state your name) *accept that everything is magnificent. Everything that I see is magnificent.*
4. **Magnificence of Self.** Say three times, *By the law of divine grace and all that is light I* (state your name) *accept that I am magnificent.*

*Techniques for Purpose through Love*

5. **Truth.** Say three times, *By the law of divine grace, and all that is light I* (state your name) *now accept that I choose from the space of the present moment.*
6. **Presence:** Be in gratitude for your breath. Thank your breath for supporting your life. Say, *thank you, breath.* Say this at least five times as you watch your breath. Do this several times during your day. Your breath brings you into the present moment. Choose from here.

*Techniques for Purpose through Peace*

7. **Kindness to Self.** Ask yourself, *Where could I be kinder with myself?* Do that.

8. **Kindness to Others.** Ask yourself how can you be kinder to your neighbor or a coworker. Do that.

9. **Bliss.** Let go of beliefs and of any definitions you have of Bliss. Allow whatever shows up. Show gratitude. Embrace it. Celebrate what shows up.

10. **Hoops of Color.** Relax your body. Ground it. Then run hoops of color up your body from your feet to your head. Envision the hoops as if they were hula hoops or large dream catchers with a fine mesh. Each hoop is a color of the corresponding chakra and the mesh of each one becomes more refined. Go from your feet up over your head. Add a couple of extra hoops that are pearlescent in pink, gold, and silver. When you are relaxed, grounded, and the energy is moving, say, *I am love, I am light, and I am infinite.* Then notice what happens.

*Techniques for Purpose through Intention*

11. **Gift to Others.** Ask yourself this question: *What gift can I give my readers, clients, or coworkers today?* Wait. Listen and then act.

12. **Gift to Self.** Ask yourself this question: *What gift can I give my body, mind, or spirit today?* Wait. Listen and then act.

# Chapter 12 ~ Absolute Energy

*Techniques for Energy through Energy*

1. **Figure of Eight.** Move the energy in a figure of eight, like the infinity symbol. Visualize the past to the left and the future to the right. The present is in the middle. Run the energy around it.

2. **Infinity Ball.** See if you can spin the figure eight horizontally into a torus. See if you can spin the torus vertically so that it becomes a ball with a center point. All energy leads in and out at the same time. Play with it.

*Techniques for Energy through Joy*

3. **The Elevator.** Imagine that you are in an elevator. You get on at the first floor, which is happy and maybe a little joyful. As you rise up through the floors each floor is increasingly more Joyful. When you get to the top, you get out. And then you notice that there is another elevator. And you ride this one to the top also. You get out. You can't possibly imagine that there is another elevator or any more Joy. But then you see another elevator.

4. **Waterfall and Geyser.** Imagine standing in a waterfall with all the opalescent colors of the rainbow falling down on you and washing into the earth. And then a geyser comes out of the earth and pushes all the colors of the rainbow up through your feet and out of your crown and into the heavens. And then the waterfall begins to rain down on you again and goes into the center of the earth. Run the energy of the waterfall down your spine. Hold your chakras back against your spine. Breathe in as the geyser rushes up and out as the waterfall runs down. Repeat this ten times.

*Techniques for Energy through Love:*

5. **Breath of God.** Imagine that God has sent an angel down to breathe with you. Imagine the angel standing in front of you with his wings out. He then reaches down with his face and breathes out into your mouth. You breathe in. Then you breathe out and he breathes in. Soon you are breathing back and forth, with your outbreath being his inbreath and your inbreath being his outbreath. You do this for a while. Maybe five breaths.

   Then the angel asks you if you want to breathe with God. You say yes. And a large gold trumpet appears where his mouth would be. Breathe in and out from this trumpet of God as you did with the angel. The air is very rarified. Do this several times.

   Thank God and the angel for their breaths. They will thank you for your breath. Allow them to thank you.

6. **Breath of a Tree.** You can do the same exercise above but with a tree. Sit in front of a tree. Introduce yourself to it. And thank it

for breathing your exhale. It breathes your carbon dioxide. If you listen, it will thank you for your breathing its oxygen. Then you and it can breathe each other consciously. You are doing it anyway. Repeat for ten minutes.

7. **Morning Prayer**. Say the Morning Prayer and end with this: "God, how much Love can I possibly be today? Show me how much Love I am. Show me how much you Love me." And then feel, listen, and watch. Watch throughout the rest of your day for signs of Love being reflected back at you. What are some examples of where Love is being demonstrated?

8. **Journaling:** Reflect in your journal on the following questions:
   - What did I see or feel during my Morning Prayer?
   - Where did I experience Love today?
   - Where did I give Love today?
   - Did I see Love where I never saw it before?
   - What color was it?
   - What did it smell like?
   - Does Love have a taste?
   - Where is Love located in my body?

## Techniques for Energy through Intent

1. **Concertina Accordion Breath Number Two**: Do the same exercise as concertina accordion breath in chapter 6 but reverse the flow of your breaths.

2. **No Breath Accordion.** Do the same exercise without your breath that you performed in the concertina accordion breath. Expand in and out without your breath.

## Techniques for Energy through Divine Perfection

3. **Not My Simulation.** Say three times, *In the name of God and by the law of divine grace, I* (state your name) *ask that everyone else's simulation now leave.*

4. **Simulation Now Leave**. Say three times, *By the law of divine grace, I* (state your name) *ask that my own simulation now leave.*

5. **I Am Space.** Say three times, *By the law of divine grace, I* (state your name) *accept that I've always been space.*

*Techniques for Energy through Purpose*

6. **Mind as Filter.** Say, *In the name of God and all that is light, I* (state your name) *now let go of the need for my mind to filter my experiences.*

7. **Safety**. Say, *In the name of God and all that is light, I* (state your name) *am safe now. I don't need myself to have any particular experience.*

8. **Steward of Body.** Say, *In the name of God and all that is light, I* (state your name) *am a steward of my body. Body, how can I serve you?*

9. **Reflections Back.** Say, *In the name of God and all that is light, I* (state your name) *now let all these reflections go back to where they came from.*

10. **No Out or In.** Find your center and then expand out four or five feet. Then expand out to the room; then the city; then the state; then the country; then the earth, and then the universe. Or just expand out as big as the universe. Try the reverse and expand or fall into the center that is you. Then further in and further in until there is no in or out. You just are. You are space.

# APPENDIX

## Morning Prayer

Saying my Morning Prayer is how I begin all my mornings. I have done so for many years. The formalization of this prayer began when I was in Bimini in the Bahamas, but it had many less formalized predecessors before then. This prayer was inspired by St. Francis of Assisi's prayer: "Let me be an instrument of thy peace."

I ask to be an instrument or a vessel. But my prayer goes beyond being a vessel, as I already know that I am one. So, I am really asking that I might notice how much I am a vessel in any given moment. And asking is there even more than that? My surroundings are just a reflection of the state I am in—so noticing them is just noticing myself.

Today's word is *Truth*. So how much truth do I see reflected back at me, and where do I see it? I think that the day is early, and we shall see.

Each word that I ask about is featured as one of the chapters in one of my two previous books plus a couple of new words in this book. To the previous words I've added *Awareness* and *Purpose*.

My Morning Prayer currently goes like this:

> *Thank you, God, for this beautiful day. Thank you. Thank you. Thank you for this wonderful place we live. Thank you for the plants and animals that share our lives with us. And today for the wonderful ... fire in the fireplace.* (Add your own words here.)
>
> *Make me an instrument of thy peace, love, joy, beauty, harmony, grace, healing, communication, abundance,*

235

*gratitude, magic, bliss, truth, divine perfection, co-creation, breath, caring, freedom, glory, intent, laughter, magnificence, magnitude, power, presence, purpose, awareness, wisdom, and wonder.*

*What shall I notice today?*

*What shall I be so much of that everything reflects it back to me; so much that I stand in awe of my own being? I listen. And I hear, "Truth." Today my word is "Truth."*

I start with gratitude for the day and for all things. The deeper I go into gratitude, the greater the experience becomes. I know that all magic starts with the catalyst of gratitude, no matter what the day looks like. A gorgeous sunrise makes it easy to be thankful. So, I usually start there, because it is easy.

Often, it is rainy, cloudy, cold, or windy. I am still grateful. Today, it is four degrees below zero. I am grateful. I am grateful to be sitting in front of the fireplace, warmed by the glow of the embers, writing this book.

# RESOURCES

## Books

*The 7 Essential Stories Charismatic Leaders Tell,* Tharakan Kurian, Best Seller Publishing, LLC. Kindle Edition, 2019.

*Beyond Biocentrism,* Robert Lanza, MD with Bob Berman, BenBella Books, 2017.

*The Force Can Be With You,* Stephen Hawley Martin, www.OakleaPress.com, 2020.

*The Holographic Universe,* Michael Talbot, Harper Perennial, 1995.

*The Magic,* Rhonda Byrne, Atria Books, 2012.

*The Secret,* Ronda Byrne, Atria Books, 2006.

## Other

*Spreading Like Wildflowers, A Sonic Bouquet from Colorado,* produced by Peter May from The Sonic Apothecary, Nature Fusion Music, 2017.

## Spiritual Practitioners

**Darius Barazandeh:** Darius founded the You Wealth Revolution, an enlightened education, and broadcasting community dedicated to helping people connect to their joy, genius, and gifts.

**Leslie Sandra Black:** Leslie is the founder of Heart Awakening.

**Katrina Chaudoir:** Katrina is an intuitive, and facilitator of visionary exploration an expanded state of consciousness; katrinalucialight@gmail.com; www.LuciaLightExperience.com

**Nikole Kadel:** Nikole is a facilitator of spiritual expansion. She leads mystical, dynamic excursions that allow people to connect with nature in such places as Bali and Tonga.

**Matt Kahn:** Matt is the author of the best-selling books *Everything Is Here to help You,* and *Whatever Arises, Love That.* He is a spiritual teacher and a highly-attuned empathic healer who has become a YouTube sensation with his healing and often humorous videos.

**Jennifer McLean:** Jennifer has served as a spiritual catalyst and healing facilitator, guiding thousands to transmute their deepest fears, blocks, and old beliefs into new levels of alignment, growth, health, wholeness, and abundance; mcleanmasterworks.com

**Zach Rehder:** Zach is an international speaker, teacher, and healer. He supports others in their awakening process. He is a facilitator of breathwork.

**Rikka Zimmerman:** Rikka is a global leader in consciousness, the creator of Adventure in Oneness LLC. She is also a singer and songwriter. She integrates unique toning techniques designed to shift the listener into a higher vibrational and energetic alignment.

## Breath Practitioners

**Zach Rehder:** www.zachrehder.com
**Rosanna Lo Meo Peachy:** www.NewBeginningsWithRosanna.com
**Fiorella Garibaldi:** www.fiorellagaribaldi.com

# ABOUT THE AUTHOR

Tricia is an architect and a Life Transformed Coach. Her life has centered on teaching, architecture, introspection, travel, storytelling, and horses.

Tricia received a BA from Macalester College in Minnesota, a BED in environmental design and architecture from the University of Minnesota, and a MOB in business from Silver Lake College in Wisconsin. She has spent a lifetime of inner awakening brought about by experiences in the Peace Corps, living and working in exotic places including Micronesia, Polynesia, Spain, and China, and traveling to sacred places such as Machu Picchu, Bimini, Sedona, Kona, and Nan Madol.

Through the years, she has made contributions to environmental protection, sustainable architecture, and education. She established Silver Creek Designs LLC as an architecture company specializing in sustainable and sacred architecture. She is an author, speaker, and life coach. She currently lives in Wisconsin with her husband of fifty-plus years, two cats, and six horses.

Contact Tricia at silvercreekdesigns@gmail.com.
Her website is at triciajeanecroyle.com

CPSIA information can be obtained
at www.ICGtesting.com
Printed in the USA
BVHW081026020720
582816BV00001B/73

9 781982 248307